The Passion
of
Jesus Christ

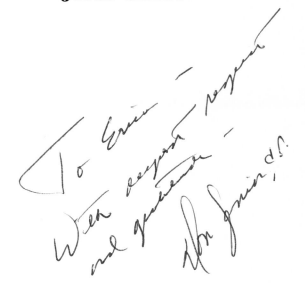

THE PASSION
OF
JESUS CHRIST

GOSPELS AND COMMENTARY

By

Donald Senior, C.P.

PASSIONIST PUBLICATIONS
UNION CITY, N.J.

The Scripture quotations are reproduced with permission from the New Testament of the *New American Bible* © 1986 by the Confraternity of Christian Doctrine, Washington, DC. All rights reserved.

Picture credits:
Edward Griswold 76
Victor Hoagland C.P. 70, 74, 76, 77, 80, 81, 85
Erich Lessing/Art Resource, NY 89
Michael Moran C.P. 40, 46, 54, 60, 87
Thomas Quinn S.J. 71, 91, 92
Zev Radovan 83, 86
Raymond Rugarber 69
Lou Schmidt 73, 81, 82, 90, 93
James Williamson 75, 79, 84
Jill T. Whitson 86, 88
The Flagellation in the Presence of Mary, Rosen-wald Collection, @ 1996 Board of Trustees, National Gallery of Art, Washington 94
St. Bridget, Rosenwald Collection, @ 1996 Board of Trustees, National Gallery of Art, Washington 95

Cover Art: Duk Soon

(T-632)

CONTENTS

Part 3

In Search of the Passion of Jesus: History, Archeology and Devotion .69

PREFACE

The passion of Jesus is both a historical event rooted in the past and a living dynamic memory that gives meaning to the present.

As past event, the passion of Jesus took place sometime around the year thirty A. D. in the turbulent world of first century Palestinian Judaism. Jesus, a compelling religious teacher and extraordinary healer, was arrested in Jerusalem and publicly executed by crucifixion, a Roman form of capital punishment. The Gospels portray Jesus' death as the culmination of his mission, the final act of selfless love and service that sealed a life totally committed to others. Jesus' death was a prophetic witness in the cause of God's justice. Despite opposition and hostility directed at him and his mission, Jesus remained faithful until the end and ultimately was vindicated by God's love, a love stronger than death.

But for Christian faith the passion of Jesus is not simply a heroic and poignant death confined to past history. The passion of Jesus lives on in the faith and experience of the Christian community. Through the mysterious communion of God with humanity, Jesus' sufferings continue in the suffering of every child of God, down to the present moment. The anxious and lonely elderly resident of a nursing home who turns her face to the crucifix on the wall. The parent who has suffered the unspeakable loss of a child who sinks to his knees like Jesus in Gethsemane. The refugee who has lost home and family to insane and inexplicable violence and cries out with Jesus, "My God, my God, why have you abandoned me?" The leader who under the threat of death tells the truth about a despotic regime while remembering that Jesus the prophet set his face for Jerusalem. The nurse who wipes sweat from the brow of an AIDS patient and sees there the face of the crucified Jesus.

The passion of Jesus is indeed a historical event that ultimately gave meaning and force to the entire mission of Jesus and it is a living memory, a powerful grace that gives meaning and hope to all human suffering. The Gospel accounts of the passion embrace both dimensions, rooting their narratives in the historical traditions about Jesus' last days but inviting the reader to find in the passion of Jesus the ultimate meaning of human existence and Christian commitment.

This book, too, embraces both dimensions of the passion of Jesus. It is written not for the specialist but for the thoughtful Christian who wants to know more about this compelling story. By recalling the distinctive portrayal of the suffering Jesus in each of the Gospels we invite the reader to enter deeply into the mystery of the passion and to bring one's own experience into vital contact with this core of the Christian message. This has been done by every generation of Christians in word and art and practices of piety, as the materials on the devotion to the passion recall for us. At the same time, the historical information that follows the study of the Gospel texts and the accompanying illustrations remind us that the death of Jesus was not the figment of Christian imagination but an event rooted in the complexities and tensions of first century history. The bibliography offers the reader leads to further study.

This book is the result of a partnership between me and Fr. Victor Hoagland, C.P., a brother Passionist. The passion narratives have been a life-long focus of my own work in Scripture, so I have provided the studies of the passion narratives. The entire book was Victor's idea and he has designed its layout, chosen the illustrations and assembled the materials on archaeology and history. If the book deserves credit, it belongs to him and his wonderfully creative spirit. The drawings that present scenes of the Passion are the work of Michael Moran, C.P., an artist whose inspired work is gaining attention across the country. Others too contributed their talent and time to this project: Zusanne Thomas and Barbara Lanzaron helped in its production, and Mary Ann Fitzpatrick offered editorial assistance.

As members of the Passionist religious community, it is our mission to help keep the dynamic memory of the passion of Jesus alive in the heart of the church. We offer this book to our readers in just that spirit.

Donald Senior, C.P.

The Passion of Jesus Christ
The Gospels

THE PASSION OF OUR LORD JESUS CHRIST ACCORDING TO MARK (14:1—15:47)

Fidelity and Betrayal:
The Passion Begins (14:1-11)

The Passover
and the Feast of Unleavened Bread
were to take place in two days' time.
So the chief priests and the scribes
were seeking a way
to arrest Jesus by treachery
and put him to death.
They said,
"Not during the festival,
for fear that there may be a riot
among the people."

When he was in Bethany
reclining at table
in the house of Simon the leper,
a woman came with an alabaster jar
of perfumed oil,
costly genuine spikenard.
She broke the alabaster jar
and poured it on his head.
There were some who were indignant.
"Why has there been this waste
of perfumed oil?
It could have been sold
for more than three hundred days' wages
and the money given to the poor."
They were infuriated with her.
Jesus said,
"Let her alone.
Why do you make trouble for her?
She has done a good thing for me.

The poor you will always have with you,
and whenever you wish
you can do good to them,
but you will not always have me.
She has done what she could.
She has anticipated anointing my body
for burial.
Amen, I say to you,
wherever the gospel is proclaimed
to the whole world,
what she has done will be told
in memory of her."

Then Judas Iscariot, one of the Twelve,
went off to the chief priests
to hand him over to them.
When they heard him
they were pleased
and promised to pay him money.
Then he looked for an opportunity
to hand him over.

The Final Passover (14:12-31)

On the first day
of the Feast of Unleavened Bread,
when they sacrificed the Passover Lamb,
his disciples said to him,
"Where do you want us to go and prepare
for you to eat the Passover?"
He sent two of his disciples
and said to them,
"Go into the city
and a man will meet you,
carrying a jar of water.
Follow him.
Wherever he enters,
say to the master of the house,
'The Teacher says,
"Where is my guest room
where I may eat the Passover
with my disciples?" '
Then he will show you
a large upper room furnished and ready.

Make the preparations for us there."
The disciples then went off,
entered the city,
and found it just as he had told them;
and they prepared the Passover.

When it was evening,
he came with the Twelve.
And as they reclined at table
and were eating,
Jesus said,
"Amen, I say to you,
one of you will betray me,
one who is eating with me."
They began to be distressed
and to say to him, one by one,
"Surely it is not I?"
He said to them,
"One of the Twelve,
the one who dips with me into the dish.
For the Son of Man indeed goes,
as it is written of him,
but woe to that man
by whom the Son of Man is betrayed.
It would be better for that man
if he had never been born."

While they were eating,
he took bread, said the blessing,
broke it, and gave it to them,
and said,
"Take it; this is my body."
Then he took a cup,
gave thanks, and gave it to them,
and they all drank from it.
He said to them,
"This is my blood of the covenant,
which will be shed for many.
Amen, I say to you,
I shall not drink again
the fruit of the vine
until the day when I drink it new
in the kingdom of God."
Then, after singing a hymn,
they went out to the Mount of Olives.

Then Jesus said to them,
"All of you will have your faith shaken,
for it is written:
'I will strike the shepherd,
and the sheep will be dispersed.'
But after I have been raised up,
I shall go before you to Galilee."
Peter said to him,
"Even though all should have their faith
    shaken,
mine will not be."
Then Jesus said to him,
"Amen, I say to you,
this very night
before the cock crows twice
you will deny me three times."
But he vehemently replied,
"Even though I should have to die with
    you,
I will not deny you."
And they all spoke similarly.

**Gethsemane: Prayer and Arrest
(14:32-52)**

Then they came to a place
named Gethsemane,
and he said to his disciples,
"Sit here while I pray."
He took with him Peter, James, and
    John,
and began to be troubled and distressed.
Then he said to them,
"My soul is sorrowful even to death.
Remain here and keep watch."

He advanced a little
and fell to the ground
and prayed that if it were possible
the hour might pass by him;
he said,
"Abba, Father,
all things are possible to you.
Take this cup away from me,
but not what I will but what you will."

When he returned he found them asleep.
He said to Peter,
"Simon, are you asleep?
Could you not keep watch for one hour?
Watch and pray
that you may not undergo the test.
The spirit is willing
but the flesh is weak."
Withdrawing again, he prayed,
saying the same thing.
Then he returned once more
and found them asleep,
for they could not keep their eyes open
and did not know what to answer him.
He returned a third time
and said to them,
"Are you still sleeping
and taking your rest?
It is enough.
The hour has come.
Behold, the Son of Man is to be
handed over to sinners.
Get up, let us go.
See, my betrayer is at hand."

Then, while he was still speaking,
Judas, one of the Twelve, arrived,
accompanied by a crowd
with swords and clubs
who had come from the chief priests,
the scribes, and the elders.
His betrayer had arranged a signal
with them, saying,
"The man I shall kiss is the one;
arrest him and lead him away securely."
He came and immediately went over to
    him
and said, "Rabbi."
And he kissed him.

At this they laid hands on him
and arrested him.
One of the bystanders drew his sword,
struck the high priest's servant,
and cut off his ear.
Jesus said to them in reply,
"Have you come out
as against a robber,
with swords and clubs, to seize me?
Day after day I was with you
teaching in the temple area,
yet you did not arrest me;
but that the scriptures
may be fulfilled."
And they all left him and fled.
Now a young man followed him
wearing nothing but a linen cloth
about his body.
They seized him,
but he left the cloth behind
and ran off naked.

**Jesus before the Sanhedrin
(14:53-72)**
They led Jesus away to the high priest,
and all the chief priests
and the elders and the scribes
came together.
Peter followed him at a distance
into the high priest's courtyard
and was seated with the guards,
warming himself at the fire.

The chief priests and the entire San-
    hedrin
kept trying to obtain testimony
against Jesus
in order to put him to death,
but they found none.
Many gave false witness against him,
but their testimony did not agree.
Some took the stand
and testified falsely against him,
alleging,
"We heard him say,
'I will destroy this temple
made with hands
and within three days I will build

another not made with hands.' "
Even so their testimony did not agree.

The high priest rose before the assembly
and questioned Jesus, saying,
"Have you no answer?
What are these men testifying
against you?"
But he was silent and answered nothing.
Again the high priest asked him
and said to him,
"Are you the Messiah,
the son of the Blessed One?"
Then Jesus answered,
"I am;
and 'you will see the Son of Man
seated at the right hand of the Power
and coming with the clouds of heaven.' "

At that the high priest tore his garments
and said,
"What further need have we of wit-
   nesses?
You have heard the blasphemy.
What do you think?"
They all condemned him
as deserving to die.
Some began to spit on him.
They blindfolded him and struck him
and said to him, "Prophesy!"
And the guards greeted him with blows.

While Peter was below in the courtyard,
one of the high priest's maids came
   along.
Seeing Peter warming himself,
she looked intently at him and said,
"You too were with the Nazarene,
   Jesus."
But he denied it saying,
"I neither know nor understand
what you are talking about."
So he went out into the outer court.
[Then the cock crowed.]

The maid saw him
and began again to say to the by-
   standers,
"This man is one of them."
Once again he denied it.
A little later
the bystanders said to Peter once more,
"Surely you are one of them;
for you too are a Galilean."
He began to curse and to swear,
"I do not know this man
about whom you are talking."
And immediately a cock crowed
a second time.
Then Peter remembered the word
that Jesus had said to him,
"Before the cock crows twice
you will deny me three times."
He broke down and wept.

The Roman Trial (15:1-21)

As soon as morning came,
the chief priests with the elders
and the scribes,
that is, the whole Sanhedrin,
held a council.
They bound Jesus,
led him away,
and handed him over to Pilate.
Pilate questioned him,
"Are you the king of the Jews?"
He said to him in reply,
"You say so."
The chief priests accused him
of many things.
Again Pilate questioned him,
"Have you no answer?
See how many things they accuse you
   of."
Jesus gave him no further answer,
so that Pilate was amazed.

Now on the occasion of the feast
he used to release to them

one prisoner whom they requested.
A man called Barabbas was then in prison
along with the rebels
who had committed murder in a rebellion.
The crowd came forward
and began to ask him
to do for them as he was accustomed.
Pilate answered,
"Do you want me to release to you
the king of the Jews?"
For he knew that it was out of envy
that the chief priests had handed him over.
But the chief priests stirred up the crowd
to have him release Barabbas
for them instead.
Pilate again said to them in reply,
"Then what [do you want] me to do
with [the man you call]
the king of the Jews?"
They shouted again,
"Crucify him."
Pilate said to them,
"Why? What evil has he done?"
They only shouted the louder,
"Crucify him."
So Pilate, wishing to satisfy the crowd,
released Barabbas to them
and, after he had Jesus scourged,
handed him over to be crucified.

The soldiers led him away
inside the palace,
that is, the praetorium,
and assembled the whole cohort.
They clothed him in purple
and, weaving a crown of thorns,
placed it on him.
They began to salute him with,
"Hail, King of the Jews!"
and kept striking his head with a reed
and spitting upon him.

They knelt before him in homage.
And when they had mocked him,
they stripped him of the purple cloak,
dressed him in his own clothes,
and led him out to crucify him.

They pressed into service a passer-by,
Simon, a Cyrenian,
who was coming in from the country,
the father of Alexander and Rufus,
to carry his cross.

Crucifixion (15:22-47)

They brought him to the place of Golgotha
(which is translated Place of the Skull).
They gave him wine drugged with myrrh,
but he did not take it.
Then they crucified him
and divided his garments
by casting lots for them
to see what each should take.

It was nine o'clock in the morning
when they crucified him.
The inscription of the charge against him read,
"The King of the Jews."
With him
they crucified two revolutionaries,
one on his right and one on his left.
Those passing by reviled him,
shaking their heads and saying,
"Aha! You who would destroy the temple
and rebuild it in three days,
save yourself by coming down
from the cross."
Likewise the chief priests,
with the scribes,
mocked him among themselves
and said,
"He saved others;

he cannot save himself.
Let the Messiah, the King of Israel,
come down now from the cross
that we may see and believe."
Those who were crucified with him
also kept abusing him.

At noon darkness came over the whole
    land
until three in the afternoon.
And at three o'clock
Jesus cried out in a loud voice,
"Eloi, Eloi, lema sabachthani?"
which is translated,
"My God, my God,
why have you forsaken me?"
Some of the bystanders who heard it
    said,
"Look, he is calling Elijah."
One of them ran,
soaked a sponge with wine,
put it on a reed,
and gave it to him to drink, saying,
"Wait, let us see
if Elijah comes to take him down."
Jesus gave a loud cry
and breathed his last.
The veil of the sanctuary was torn
in two from top to bottom.
When the centurion who stood facing
    him
saw how he breathed his last
he said,
"Truly this man was the Son of God!"
There were also women
looking on from a distance.
Among them were Mary Magdalene,

Mary the mother of the younger James
and of Joses,
and Salome.
These women had followed him
when he was in Galilee
and ministered to him.
There were also many other women
who had come up with him to Jerusa-
    lem.

When it was already evening,
since it was the day of preparation,
the day before the sabbath,
Joseph of Arimathea,
a distinguished member of the council,
who was himself awaiting
the kingdom of God,
came and courageously went to Pilate
and asked for the body of Jesus.
Pilate was amazed
that he was already dead.
He summoned the centurion
and asked him
if Jesus had already died.
And when he learned of it
from the centurion,
he gave the body to Joseph.
Having bought a linen cloth,
he took him down,
wrapped him in the linen cloth
and laid him in a tomb
that had been hewn out of the rock.
Then he rolled a stone
against the entrance of the tomb.
Mary Magdalene
and Mary the mother of Joses
watched where he was laid.

THE PASSION OF OUR LORD JESUS CHRIST ACCORDING TO MATTHEW (26:1—27:66)

The Gathering Storm (26:1-16)

When Jesus finished all these words,
he said to his disciples,
"You know that in two days' time
it will be Passover,
and the Son of Man will be handed over
to be crucified."
Then the chief priests
and the elders of the people
assembled in the palace of the high priest,
who was called Caiaphas,
and they consulted together
to arrest Jesus by treachery
and put him to death.
But they said,
"Not during the festival,
that there may not be a riot
among the people."

Now when Jesus was in Bethany
in the house of Simon the leper,
a woman came up to him
with an alabaster jar
of costly perfumed oil,
and poured it on his head
while he was reclining at table.
When the disciples saw this,
they were indignant and said,
"Why this waste?
It could have been sold for much,
and the money given to the poor."
Since Jesus knew this,
he said to them,

"Why do you make trouble for the
woman?
She has done a good thing for me.
The poor you will always have with you;
but you will not always have me.
In pouring this perfumed oil
upon my body,
she did it to prepare me for burial.
Amen, I say to you,
wherever this gospel is proclaimed
in the whole world,
what she has done will be spoken of,
in memory of her."

Then one of the Twelve,
who was called Judas Iscariot,
went to the chief priests and said,
"What are you willing to give me
if I hand him over to you?"
They paid him thirty pieces of silver,
and from that time on
he looked for an opportunity
to hand him over.

The Kairos (26:17-35)

On the first day
of the Feast of Unleavened Bread,
the disciples approached Jesus and said,
"Where do you want us
to prepare for you to eat the Passover?"
He said,
"Go into the city to a certain man
and tell him,
'The Teacher says,
"My appointed time draws near;
in your house
I shall celebrate the Passover
with my disciples." ' "
The disciples then did
as Jesus had ordered,
and prepared the Passover.

When it was evening,
he reclined at table with the Twelve.

And while they were eating, he said,
"Amen, I say to you,
one of you will betray me."
Deeply distressed at this,
they began to say to him
one after another,
"Surely it is not I, Lord?"
He said in reply,
"He who has dipped his hand
into the dish with me
is the one who will betray me.
The Son of Man indeed goes,
as it is written of him,
but woe to that man by whom
the Son of Man is betrayed.
It would be better for that man
if he had never been born."
Then Judas, his betrayer, said in reply,
"Surely it is not I, Rabbi?"
He answered,
"You have said so."

While they were eating,
Jesus took bread,
said the blessing,
broke it,
and giving it to his disciples said,
"Take and eat;
this is my body."
Then he took a cup,
gave thanks,
and gave it to them, saying,
"Drink from it, all of you,
for this is my blood of the covenant,
which will be shed on behalf of many
for the forgiveness of sins.
I tell you,
from now on
I shall not drink this fruit of the vine
until the day
when I drink it with you new
in the kingdom of my Father."
Then, after singing a hymn,
they went out to the Mount of Olives.

Then Jesus said to them,
"This night all of you
will have your faith in me shaken,
for it is written:
'I will strike the shepherd,
and the sheep of the flock will be dis-
    persed';
but after I have been raised up,
I shall go before you to Galilee."
Peter said to him in reply,
"Though all may have their faith in you
    shaken,
mine will never be."
Jesus said to him,
"Amen, I say to you,
this very night before the cock crows,
you will deny me three times."
Peter said to him,
"Even though I should have to die
with you,
I will not deny you."
And all the disciples spoke likewise.

Gethsemane (26:36-56)

Then Jesus came with them
to a place called Gethsemane,
and he said to his disciples,
"Sit here while I go over there and pray."
He took along Peter
and the two sons of Zebedee,
and began to feel sorrow and distress.
Then he said to them,
"My soul is sorrowful even to death.
Remain here and keep watch with me."
He advanced a little
and fell prostrate in prayer, saying,
"My Father,
if it is possible,
let this cup pass from me;
yet, not as I will,
but as you will."
When he returned to his disciples
he found them asleep.

He said to Peter,
"So you could not keep watch with me
for one hour?
Watch and pray
that you may not undergo the test.
The spirit is willing,
but the flesh is weak."

Withdrawing a second time,
he prayed again,
"My Father,
if it is not possible that this cup pass
without my drinking it,
your will be done!"
Then he returned once more
and found them asleep,
for they could not keep their eyes open.
He left them and withdrew again
and prayed a third time,
saying the same thing again.
Then he returned to his disciples
and said to them,
"Are you still sleeping
and taking your rest?
Behold, the hour is at hand
when the Son of Man is to be handed
    over to sinners.
Get up, let us go.
Look, my betrayer is at hand."

While he was still speaking,
Judas, one of the Twelve, arrived,
accompanied by a large crowd,
with swords and clubs,
who had come from the chief priests
and the elders of the people.
His betrayer had arranged
a sign with them, saying,
"The man I shall kiss is the one;
arrest him."
Immediately he went over to Jesus
and said, "Hail, Rabbi!"
and he kissed him.
Jesus answered him,

"Friend, do what you have come for."
Then stepping forward they laid hands
on Jesus
and arrested him.
And behold,
one of those who accompanied Jesus
put his hand to his sword,
drew it,
and struck the high priest's servant,
cutting off his ear.

Then Jesus said to him,
"Put your sword back into its sheath,
for all who take the sword
will perish by the sword.
Do you think
that I cannot call upon my Father
and he will not provide me
at this moment
with more than twelve legions of angels?
But then how would the scriptures be
    fulfilled
which say that it must come to pass
in this way?"
At that hour Jesus said to the crowds,
"Have you come out as against a robber,
with swords and clubs to seize me?
Day after day I sat teaching
in the temple area,
yet you did not arrest me.
But all this has come to pass
that the writings of the prophets may be
    fulfilled."
Then all the disciples left him and fled.

Jesus on Trial (26:57—27:10)

Those who had arrested Jesus led him
    away
to Caiaphas the high priest,
where the scribes and the elders were
    assembled.
Peter was following him at a distance
as far as the high priest's courtyard,
and going inside he sat down

with the servants
to see the outcome.
The chief priests and the entire San-
    hedrin
kept trying to obtain false testimony
against Jesus
in order to put him to death,
but they found none,
though many false witnesses came for-
    ward.
Finally two came forward who stated,
"This man said,
'I can destroy the temple of God
and within three days rebuild it.' "

The high priest rose and addressed him,
"Have you no answer?
What are these men testifying against
    you?"
But Jesus was silent.
Then the high priest said to him,
"I order you to tell us under oath
before the living God
whether you are the Messiah,
the Son of God."
Jesus said to him in reply,
"You have said so.
But I tell you:
From now on you will see 'the Son of
    Man
seated at the right hand of the Power'
and 'coming on the clouds of heaven.' "
Then the high priest tore his robes
and said,
"He has blasphemed!
What further need have we of wit-
    nesses?
You have now heard the blasphemy;
what is your opinion?"
They said in reply,
"He deserves to die!"
Then they spat in his face
and struck him,
while some slapped him, saying,

"Prophesy for us, Messiah:
who is it that struck you?"

Now Peter was sitting outside
in the courtyard.
One of the maids came over to him
and said,
"You too were with Jesus the Galilean."
But he denied it in front of everyone,
saying,
"I do not know what you are talking
    about!"
As he went out to the gate,
another girl saw him
and said to those who were there,
"This man was with Jesus the Na-
    zorean."
Again he denied it with an oath,
"I do not know the man!"
A little later the bystanders came over
and said to Peter,
"Surely you too are one of them;
even your speech gives you away."
At that he began to curse and to swear,
"I do not know the man."
And immediately a cock crowed.
Then Peter remembered the word
that Jesus had spoken:
"Before the cock crows
you will deny me three times."
He went out and began to weep bitterly.

When it was morning,
all the chief priests
and the elders of the people
took counsel against Jesus
to put him to death.
They bound him,
led him away,
and handed him over to Pilate, the gov-
    ernor.
Then Judas, his betrayer,
seeing that Jesus had been condemned,
deeply regretted what he had done.

He returned the thirty pieces of silver
to the chief priests and elders,
saying,
"I have sinned
in betraying innocent blood."
They said,
"What is that to us?
Look to it yourself."
Flinging the money into the temple,
he departed
and went off and hanged himself.
The chief priests gathered up the money,
but said,
"It is not lawful to deposit this
in the temple treasury,
for it is the price of blood."
After consultation,
they used it to buy the potter's field
as a burial place for foreigners.
That is why that field even today
is called the Field of Blood.
Then was fulfilled what had been said
through Jeremiah the prophet,
"And they took the thirty pieces
of silver,
the value of a man with a price
on his head,
a price set by some of the Israelites,
and they paid it out
for the potter's field
just as the Lord had commanded me."

The Messiah Condemned (27:11-32)

Now Jesus stood before the governor,
and he questioned him,
"Are you the king of the Jews?"
Jesus said,
"You say so."
And when he was accused
by the chief priests and elders,
he made no answer.
Then Pilate said to him,
"Do you not hear how many things
they are testifying against you?"
But he did not answer him one word,
so that the governor was greatly
    amazed.

Now on the occasion of the feast
the governor was accustomed
to release to the crowd one prisoner
whom they wished.
And at that time
they had a notorious prisoner
called [Jesus] Barabbas.
So when they had assembled,
Pilate said to them,
"Which one do you want me
to release to you,
[Jesus] Barabbas,
or Jesus called Messiah?"
For he knew that it was out of envy
that they had handed him over.
While he was still seated on the bench,
his wife sent him a message,
"Have nothing to do
with that righteous man.
I suffered much in a dream today
because of him."

The chief priests and the elders
persuaded the crowds
to ask for Barabbas
but to destroy Jesus.
The governor said to them in reply,
"Which of the two
do you want me to release to you?"
They answered,
"Barabbas!"
Pilate said to them,
"Then what shall I do with Jesus
called Messiah?"
They all said,
"Let him be crucified!"
But he said,
"Why? What evil has he done?"
They only shouted the louder,

"Let him be crucified!"
When Pilate saw
that he was not succeeding at all,
but that a riot was breaking out instead,
he took water and washed his hands
in the sight of the crowd,
saying,
"I am innocent of this man's blood.
Look to it yourselves."
And the whole people said in reply,
"His blood be upon us
and upon our children."
Then he released Barabbas to them,
but after he had Jesus scourged,
he handed him over to be crucified.

Then the soldiers of the governor
took Jesus inside the praetorium
and gathered the whole cohort
around him.
They stripped off his clothes
and threw a scarlet military cloak
about him.
Weaving a crown out of thorns,
they placed it on his head,
and a reed in his right hand.
And kneeling before him,
they mocked him, saying,
"Hail, King of the Jews!"
They spat upon him
and took the reed and kept striking him
on the head.
And when they had mocked him,
they stripped him of the cloak,
dressed him in his own clothes,
and led him off to crucify him.
As they were going out,
they met a Cyrenian named Simon;
this man they pressed into service
to carry his cross.

The Dawn of the New Age (27:33-66)

And when they came to a place
called Golgotha

(which means Place of the Skull),
they gave Jesus wine to drink
mixed with gall.
But when he had tasted it,
he refused to drink.
After they had crucified him,
they divided his garments
by casting lots;
then they sat down
and kept watch over him there.
And they placed over his head
the written charge against him:
This is Jesus, the King of the Jews.
Two revolutionaries were crucified
with him,
one on his right
and the other on his left.
Those passing by reviled him,
shaking their heads and saying,
"You who would destroy the temple
and rebuild it in three days,
save yourself,
if you are the Son of God,
[and] come down from the cross!"
Likewise the chief priests
with the scribes and elders
mocked him and said,
"He saved others;
he cannot save himself.
So he is the king of Israel!
Let him come down from the cross now,
and we will believe in him.
He trusted in God;
let him deliver him now
if he wants him.
For he said,
'I am the Son of God.' "
The revolutionaries
who were crucified with him
also kept abusing him in the same way.

From noon onward,
darkness came over the whole land
until three in the afternoon.

And about three o'clock
Jesus cried out in a loud voice,
"Eli, Eli, lema sabachthani?"
which means,
"My God, my God,
why have you forsaken me?"
Some of the bystanders who heard it said,
"This one is calling for Elijah."
Immediately one of them ran
to get a sponge;
he soaked it in wine,
and putting it on a reed,
gave it to him to drink.
But the rest said,
"Wait,
let us see if Elijah comes to save him."
But Jesus cried out again
in a loud voice,
and gave up his spirit.

And behold, the veil of the sanctuary
was torn in two from top to bottom.
The earth quaked,
rocks were split,
tombs were opened,
and the bodies of many saints
who had fallen asleep
were raised.
And coming forth from their tombs
after his resurrection,
they entered the holy city
and appeared to many.
The centurion and the men with him
who were keeping watch over Jesus
feared greatly when they saw
the earthquake and all that was happen-
   ing,
and they said,
"Truly, this was the Son of God!"

There were many women there,
looking on from a distance,
who had followed Jesus from Galilee,
ministering to him.
Among them were Mary Magdalene
and Mary the mother of James and
   Joseph,
and the mother of the sons of Zebedee.

When it was evening,
there came a rich man from Arimathea
named Joseph,
who was himself a disciple of Jesus.
He went to Pilate
and asked for the body of Jesus;
then Pilate ordered it to be handed over.
Taking the body,
Joseph wrapped it [in] clean linen
and laid it in his new tomb
that he had hewn in the rock.
Then he rolled a huge stone
across the entrance to the tomb
and departed.
But Mary Magdalene and the other Mary
remained sitting there,
facing the tomb.

The next day,
the one following the day of preparation,
the chief priests and the Pharisees
gathered before Pilate and said,
"Sir, we remember that this imposter
while still alive
said,
'After three days I will be raised up.'
Give orders, then,
that the grave be secured
until the third day,
lest his disciples come and steal him
and say to the people,
'He has been raised from the dead.'
This last imposture would be worse
than the first."
Pilate said to them,
"The guard is yours;
go secure it as best you can."
So they went and secured the tomb
by fixing a seal to the stone
and setting the guard.

THE PASSION OF OUR LORD JESUS CHRIST ACCORDING TO LUKE (22:1—23:56)

The Last Supper (22:1-38)

Now the feast of Unleavened Bread,
called the Passover,
was drawing near,
and the chief priests and the scribes
were seeking a way to put him to death,
for they were afraid of the people.
Then Satan entered into Judas,
the one surnamed Iscariot,
who was counted among the Twelve,
and he went to the chief priests
and temple guards
to discuss a plan
for handing him over to them.
They were pleased
and agreed to pay him money.
He accepted their offer
and sought a favorable opportunity
to hand him over to them
in the absence of a crowd.

When the day of the Feast of Unleavened Bread arrived,
the day for sacrificing the Passover Lamb,
he sent out Peter and John,
instructing them,
"Go and make preparations
for us to eat the Passover."
They asked him,
"Where do you want us
to make the preparations?"
And he answered them,

"When you go into the city,
a man will meet you
carrying a jar of water.
Follow him into the house that he enters
and say to the master of the house,
'The Teacher says to you,
"Where is the guest room
where I may eat the Passover
with my disciples?" '
He will show you a large upper room
that is furnished.
Make the preparations there."
Then they went off and found everything
exactly as he had told them,
and there they prepared the Passover.

When the hour came,
he took his place at table
with the apostles.
He said to them,
"I have eagerly desired
to eat this Passover with you
before I suffer,
for, I tell you,
I shall not eat it [again]
until there is fulfillment
in the kingdom of God."

Then he took a cup,
gave thanks, and said,
"Take this and share it among yourselves;
for I tell you [that] from this time on
I shall not drink of the fruit
of the vine
until the kingdom of God comes."

Then he took the bread,
said the blessing,
broke it,
and gave it to them, saying,
"This is my body,
which will be given for you;
do this in memory of me."
And likewise the cup
after they had eaten, saying,

"This cup is the new covenant
in my blood,
which will be shed for you.
And yet behold,
the hand of the one who is to betray me
is with me on the table;
for the Son of Man indeed goes
as it has been determined;
but woe to that man
by whom he is betrayed."
And they began to debate among them-
    selves
who among them would do such a deed.

Then an argument broke out among them
about which of them should be regarded
as the greatest.
He said to them,
"The kings of the Gentiles lord it over
    them
and those in authority over them
are addressed as 'Benefactors';
but among you it shall not be so.
Rather, let the greatest among you be
as the youngest,
and the leader as the servant.
For who is greater:
the one seated at table
or the one who serves?
Is it not the one seated at table?
I am among you as the one who serves.
It is you who have stood by me
in my trials;
and I confer a kingdom on you,
just as my Father has conferred one
on me,
that you may eat and drink at my table
in my kingdom;
and you will sit on thrones
judging the twelve tribes of Israel.

"Simon, Simon,
behold Satan has demanded
to sift all of you like wheat,
but I have prayed

that your own faith may not fail;
and once you have turned back,
you must strengthen your brothers."
He said to him,
"Lord, I am prepared to go to prison
and to die with you."
But he replied,
"I tell you, Peter,
before the cock crows this day,
you will deny three times
that you know me."

He said to them,
"When I sent you forth
without a money bag or a sack or sandals,
were you in need of anything?"
"No, nothing,"
they replied.
He said to them,
"But now one who has a money bag
should take it,
and likewise a sack,
and one who does not have a sword
should sell his cloak and buy one.
For I tell you
that this scripture must be fulfilled in
    me, namely,
'He was counted among the wicked';
and indeed what is written about me
is coming to fulfillment."
Then they said,
"Lord, look, there are two swords here."
But he replied,
"It is enough!"

The Hour of Darkness (22:39-65)

Then going out he went,
as was his custom,
to the Mount of Olives,
and the disciples followed him.
When he arrived at the place
he said to them,
"Pray that you may not undergo the test."
After withdrawing about a stone's throw
from them

and kneeling,
he prayed, saying,
"Father, if you are willing,
take this cup away from me;
still, not my will but yours be done."
[And to strengthen him
an angel from heaven appeared to him.
He was in such agony
and he prayed so fervently
that his sweat became like drops of blood
falling upon the ground.]

When he rose from prayer
and returned to his disciples,
he found them sleeping from grief.
He said to them,
"Why are you sleeping?
Get up and pray
that you may not undergo the test."

While he was still speaking,
a crowd approached
and in front was one of the Twelve,
a man named Judas.
He went up to Jesus to kiss him.
Jesus said to him,
"Judas, are you betraying the Son of Man
with a kiss?"
His disciples realized
what was about to happen,
and they asked,
"Lord, shall we strike with a sword?"
And one of them struck the high priest's
    servant
and cut off his right ear.
But Jesus said in reply,
"Stop, no more of this!"
Then he touched the servant's ear
and healed him.
And Jesus said to the chief priests
and temple guards and elders
who had come for him,
"Have you come out as against a robber,
with swords and clubs?
Day after day

I was with you in the temple area,
and you did not seize me;
but this is your hour,
the time for the power of darkness."

After arresting him they led him away
and took him to the house
of the high priest;
Peter was following at a distance.
They lit a fire
in the middle of the courtyard
and sat around it,
and Peter sat down with them.
When a maid saw him seated in the light,
she looked intently at him and said,
"This man too was with him."
But he denied it saying,
"Woman, I do not know him."
A short while later someone else saw him
and said,
"You too are one of them";
but Peter answered,
"My friend, I am not."
About an hour later,
still another insisted,
"Assuredly, this man too was with him,
for he also is a Galilean."
But Peter said,
"My friend, I do not know
what you are talking about."

Just as he was saying this,
the cock crowed,
and the Lord turned and looked at Peter;
and Peter remembered the word of the
    Lord,
how he had said to him,
"Before the cock crows today,
you will deny me three times."
He went out and began to weep bitterly.

The men who held Jesus in custody
were ridiculing and beating him.
They blindfolded him
and questioned him, saying,

"Prophesy! Who is it that struck you?"
And they reviled him
in saying many other things against him.

Jesus on Trial (22:66—23:25)

When day came
the council of elders of the people met,
both chief priests and scribes,
and they brought him
before their Sanhedrin.
They said,
"If you are the Messiah, tell us,"
but he replied to them,
"If I tell you,
you will not believe,
and if I question,
you will not respond.
But from this time on
the Son of Man will be seated
at the right hand of the power of God."

They all asked,
"Are you then the Son of God?"
He replied to them,
"You say that I am."
Then they said,
"What further need have we for testi-
    mony?
We have heard it from his own mouth."

Then the whole assembly of them arose
and brought him before Pilate.
They brought charges against him,
saying,
"We found this man misleading our peo-
    ple;
he opposes the payment of taxes
to Caesar
and maintains that he is the Messiah,
a king."
Pilate asked him,
"Are you the king of the Jews?"
He said to him in reply,
"You say so."

Pilate then addressed the chief priests
and the crowds,
"I find this man not guilty."
But they were adamant and said,
"He is inciting the people
with his teaching
throughout all Judea,
from Galilee where he began
even to here."

On hearing this
Pilate asked if the man was a Galilean;
and upon learning
that he was under Herod's jurisdiction,
he sent him to Herod
who was in Jerusalem at that time.
Herod was very glad to see Jesus;
he had been wanting to see him
for a long time,
for he had heard about him
and had been hoping
to see him perform some sign.
He questioned him at length,
but he gave him no answer.
The chief priests and scribes,
meanwhile, stood by accusing him
    harshly.
[Even] Herod and his soldiers
treated him contemptuously
and mocked him,
and after clothing him
in resplendent garb,
he sent him back to Pilate.
Herod and Pilate became friends
that very day,
even though they had been enemies for-
    merly.

Pilate then summoned the chief priests,
the rulers, and the people
and said to them,
"You brought this man to me
and accused him
of inciting the people to revolt.
I have conducted my investigation

in your presence
and have not found this man guilty
of the charges you have brought
against him,
nor did Herod,
for he sent him back to us.
So no capital crime has been committed
by him.
Therefore I shall have him flogged
and then release him."

But all together they shouted out,
"Away with this man!
Release Barabbas to us."
(Now Barabbas had been imprisoned
for a rebellion
that had taken place in the city
and for murder.)
Again Pilate addressed them,
still wishing to release Jesus,
but they continued their shouting,
"Crucify him! Crucify him!"
Pilate addressed them a third time,
"What evil has this man done?
I found him guilty of no capital crime.
Therefore I shall have him flogged
and then release him."

With loud shouts, however,
they persisted in calling
for his crucifixion,
and their voices prevailed.
The verdict of Pilate was
that their demand should be granted.
So he released the man
who had been imprisoned
for rebellion and murder,
for whom they asked,
and he handed Jesus over to them
to deal with as they wished.

The Way of the Cross (23:26-32)

As they led him away
they took hold of a certain Simon,
a Cyrenian,
who was coming in from the country;
and after laying the cross on him,
they made him carry it behind Jesus.
A large crowd of people followed Jesus,
including many women
who mourned and lamented him.
Jesus turned to them and said,
"Daughters of Jerusalem,
do not weep for me;
weep instead for yourselves
and for your children,
for indeed, the days are coming
when people will say,
'Blessed are the barren,
the wombs that never bore
and the breasts that never nursed.'
At that time
people will say to the mountains,
'Fall upon us!'
and to the hills,
'Cover us!'
for if these things are done
when the wood is green
what will happen when it is dry?"
Now two others, both criminals,
were led away with him to be executed.

The Death of the Just Man (23:33-49)

When they came
to the place called the Skull,
they crucified him and the criminals
    there,
one on his right,
the other on his left.
[Then Jesus said,
"Father, forgive them,
they know not what they do."]
They divided his garments
by casting lots.

The people stood by and watched;
the rulers, meanwhile, sneered at him
and said,

"He saved others,
let him save himself
if he is the chosen one,
the Messiah of God."
Even the soldiers jeered at him.
As they approached to offer him wine
they called out,
"If you are the King of the Jews,
save yourself."
Above him there was an inscription
that read,
"This is the King of the Jews."

Now one of the criminals hanging there
reviled Jesus, saying,
"Are you not the Messiah?
Save yourself and us."
The other, however, rebuking him, said
in reply,
"Have you no fear of God,
for you are subject
to the same condemnation?
And indeed, we have been condemned
   justly,
for the sentence we received corresponds
to our crimes,
but this man has done nothing criminal."
Then he said,
"Jesus, remember me
when you come into your kingdom."
He replied to him,
"Amen, I say to you,
today you will be with me in Paradise."

It was now about noon
and darkness came over the whole land
until three in the afternoon
because of an eclipse of the sun.
Then the veil of the temple was torn
down the middle.
Jesus cried out in a loud voice,
"Father,
into your hands I commend my spirit";
and when he had said this
he breathed his last.

The centurion
who witnessed what had happened
glorified God and said,
"This man was innocent beyond doubt."
When all the people
who had gathered for this spectacle
saw what had happened,
they returned home beating their breasts;
but all his acquaintances stood
at a distance,
including the women
who had followed him from Galilee
and saw these events.

Death and Victory (23:50-56)

Now there was a virtuous and righteous
   man
named Joseph
who, though he was a member of the
   council,
had not consented to their plan of action.
He came from the Jewish town of Arimathea
and was awaiting the kingdom of God.
He went to Pilate
and asked for the body of Jesus.
After he had taken the body down,
he wrapped it in a linen cloth
and laid him in a rock-hewn tomb
in which no one had yet been buried.
It was the day of preparation,
and the sabbath was about to begin.

The women
who had come from Galilee with him
followed behind,
and when they had seen the tomb
and the way in which his body was laid
   in it,
they returned and prepared spices
and perfumed oils.
Then they rested on the sabbath
according to the commandment.

THE PASSION OF OUR LORD JESUS CHRIST ACCORDING TO JOHN (18:1—19:42)

The Arrest (18:1-11)

Jesus went out with his disciples
across the Kidron valley
to where there was a garden,
into which he and his disciples entered.
Judas his betrayer also knew the place,
because Jesus had often met there
with his disciples.

So Judas got
a band of soldiers and guards
from the chief priests and the Pharisees
and went there
with lanterns, torches, and weapons.

Jesus, knowing everything
that was going to happen to him,
went out and said to them,
"Whom are you looking for?"
They answered him,
"Jesus the Nazorean."
He said to them,
"I AM."

Judas his betrayer was also with them.
When he said to them, "I AM,"
they turned away and fell to the ground.
So he again asked them,
"Whom are you looking for?"
They said,
"Jesus the Nazorean."
Jesus answered,
"I told you that I AM.

So if you are looking for me,
let these men go."
This was to fulfill what he had said,
"I have not lost any
of those you gave me."

Then Simon Peter, who had a sword,
drew it,
struck the high priest's slave,
and cut off his right ear.
The slave's name was Malchus.
Jesus said to Peter,
"Put your sword into its scabbard.
Shall I not drink the cup
that the Father gave me?"

In the Courtyard of the High Priest (18:12-27)

So the band of soldiers,
the tribune, and the Jewish guards
seized Jesus,
bound him,
and brought him to Annas first.
He was the father-in-law of Caiaphas,
who was high priest that year.
It was Caiaphas
who had counseled the Jews
that it was better
that one man should die
rather than the people.

Simon Peter and another disciple
followed Jesus.
Now the other disciple was known
to the high priest,
and he entered the courtyard
of the high priest
with Jesus.
But Peter stood at the gate outside.
So the other disciple,
the acquaintance of the high priest,
went out and spoke to the gatekeeper
and brought Peter in.
Then the maid who was the gatekeeper

said to Peter,
"You are not one of this man's disciples,
are you?"
He said,
"I am not."
Now the slaves and guards were stand-
    ing
around a charcoal fire
that they had made, because it was cold,
and were warming themselves.
Peter was also standing there
keeping warm.

The high priest questioned Jesus
about his disciples
and about his doctrine.
Jesus answered him,
"I have spoken publicly to the world.
I have always taught in a synagogue
or in the temple area
where all the Jews gather,
and in secret I have said nothing.
Why ask me?
Ask those who heard me
what I said to them.
They know what I said."

When he had said this,
one of the temple guards standing there
struck Jesus and said,
"Is this the way
you answer the high priest?"
Jesus answered him,
"If I have spoken wrongly,
testify to the wrong;
but if I have spoken rightly,
why do you strike me?"
Then Annas sent him bound to Caiaphas
the high priest.

Now Simon Peter was standing there
keeping warm.
And they said to him,
"You are not one of his disciples,
are you?"
He denied it and said,
"I am not."
One of the slaves of the high priest,
a relative of the one
whose ear Peter had cut off, said,
"Didn't I see you in the garden with
    him?"
Again Peter denied it.
And immediately the cock crowed.

Jesus before Pilate (18:28-40)

Then they brought Jesus
from Caiaphas to the praetorium.
It was morning.
And they themselves did not enter
the praetorium,
in order not to be defiled
so that they could eat the Passover.
So Pilate came out to them and said,
"What charge do you bring
[against] this man?"
They answered and said to him,
"If he were not a criminal,
we would not have handed him over
to you."

At this, Pilate said to them,
"Take him yourselves,
and judge him according to your law."
The Jews answered him,
"We do not have the right
to execute anyone,"
in order that the word of Jesus
might be fulfilled that he said
indicating the kind of death
he would die.

So Pilate went back into the praetorium
and summoned Jesus and said to him,
"Are you the King of the Jews?"
Jesus answered,
"Do you say this on your own
or have others told you about me?"

Pilate answered,
"I am not a Jew, am I?
Your own nation and the chief priests
handed you over to me.
What have you done?"
Jesus answered,
"My kingdom does not belong
to this world.
If my kingdom did belong to this world,
my attendants [would] be fighting
to keep me from being handed over
to the Jews.
But as it is, my kingdom is not here."
So Pilate said to him,
"Then you are a king?"
Jesus answered,
"You say I am a king.
For this I was born
and for this I came into the world,
to testify to the truth.
Everyone who belongs to the truth
listens to my voice."
Pilate said to him,
"What is truth?"

When he had said this,
he again went out to the Jews
and said to them,
"I find no guilt in him.
But you have a custom
that I release one prisoner to you
at Passover.
Do you want me to release to you
the King of the Jews?"
They cried out again,
"Not this one but Barabbas!"
Now Barabbas was a revolutionary.

Jesus the Crucified King (19:1-16)

Then Pilate took Jesus
and had him scourged.
And the soldiers wove a crown
out of thorns
and placed it on his head,

and clothed him in a purple cloak,
and they came to him and said,
"Hail, King of the Jews!"
And they struck him repeatedly.

Once more Pilate went out
and said to them,
"Look, I am bringing him out to you,
so that you may know
that I find no guilt in him."
So Jesus came out,
wearing the crown of thorns
and the purple cloak.
And he said to them,
"Behold, the man!"

When the chief priests and the guards
    saw him
they cried out,
"Crucify him, crucify him!"
Pilate said to them,
"Take him yourselves and crucify him.
I find no guilt in him."
The Jews answered,
"We have a law,
and according to that law
he ought to die,
because he made himself
the Son of God."

Now when Pilate heard this statement,
he became even more afraid,
and went back into the praetorium
and said to Jesus,
"Where are you from?"
Jesus did not answer him.
So Pilate said to him,
"Do you not speak to me?
Do you not know
that I have power to release you
and I have power to crucify you?"
Jesus answered [him],
"You would have no power over me
if it had not been given to you

from above.
For this reason
the one who handed me over to you
has the greater sin."

Consequently, Pilate tried to release him;
but the Jews cried out,
"If you release him,
you are not a Friend of Caesar.
Everyone who makes himself a king
opposes Caesar."

When Pilate heard these words
he brought Jesus out
and seated him on the judge's bench
in the place called Stone Pavement,
in Hebrew, Gabbatha.
It was preparation day for Passover,
and it was about noon.

And he said to the Jews,
"Behold, your king!"
They cried out,
"Take him away,
take him away!
Crucify him!"
Pilate said to them,
"Shall I crucify your king?"
The chief priests answered,
"We have no king but Caesar."
Then he handed him over to them
to be crucified.

**The Lifting Up of the Son of Man
(19:17-30)**

So they took Jesus,
and carrying the cross himself
he went out to what is called
the Place of the Skull,
in Hebrew, Golgotha.
There they crucified him,
and with him two others,
one on either side,
with Jesus in the middle.

Pilate also had an inscription written
and put on the cross.
It read,
"Jesus the Nazorean,
the King of the Jews."
Now many of the Jews read this inscription,
because the place where Jesus was crucified
was near the city;
and it was written
in Hebrew, Latin, and Greek.
So the chief priests of the Jews said
to Pilate,
"Do not write
'The King of the Jews,'
but that he said,
'I am the King of the Jews.' "
Pilate answered,
"What I have written,
I have written."

When the soldiers had crucified Jesus,
they took his clothes
and divided them into four shares,
a share for each soldier.
They also took his tunic,
but the tunic was seamless,
woven in one piece from the top down.
So they said to one another,
"Let's not tear it,
but cast lots for it
to see whose it will be,"
in order that the passage of scripture
might be fulfilled
[that says]:
"They divided my garments among
them,
and for my vesture they cast lots."
This is what the soldiers did.

Standing by the cross of Jesus
were his mother and his mother's sister,
Mary the wife of Clopas,

and Mary of Magdala.
When Jesus saw his mother
and the disciple there whom he loved,
he said to his mother,
"Woman, behold, your son."
Then he said to the disciple,
"Behold, your mother."
And from that hour
the disciple took her into his home.

After this,
aware that everything was now finished,
in order that the scripture might be ful-
    filled,
Jesus said,
"I thirst."
There was a vessel filled with common
    wine.
So they put a sponge soaked in wine
on a sprig of hyssop
and put it up to his mouth.
When Jesus had taken the wine,
he said,
"It is finished."
And bowing his head,
he handed over the spirit.

Testimony (19:31-42)

Now since it was preparation day,
in order that the bodies might not re-
    main
on the cross on the sabbath,
for the sabbath day of that week
was a solemn one,
the Jews asked Pilate
that their legs be broken
and they be taken down.
So the soldiers came
and broke the legs of the first
and then of the other one
who was crucified with Jesus.
But when they came to Jesus
and saw that he was already dead,
they did not break his legs,
but one soldier thrust his lance
into his side,
and immediately
blood and water flowed out.
An eyewitness has testified,
and his testimony is true;
he knows that he is speaking the truth,
so that you also may [come to] believe.
For this happened so that
the scripture passage might be fulfilled:
"Not a bone of it will be broken."
And again another passage says:
"They will look upon him
whom they have pierced."
After this, Joseph of Arimathea,
secretly a disciple of Jesus for fear of the
    Jews,
asked Pilate if he could remove
the body of Jesus.
And Pilate permitted it.
So he came and took his body.

Nicodemus,
the one who had first come to him
at night,
also came bringing a mixture
of myrrh and aloes
weighing about one hundred pounds.
They took the body of Jesus
and bound it with burial cloths
along with spices,
according to the Jewish burial custom.
Now in the place
where he had been crucified
there was a garden,
and in that garden a new tomb,
in which no one had yet been buried.
So they laid Jesus there
because of the Jewish preparation day;
for the tomb was close by.

The Passion of Jesus Christ

Commentary on the
Passion Gospels

INTRODUCTION

The passion narratives provide the climax for each of the four gospels, catching up themes that weave their way through the evangelists' entire portrayal of Jesus' life and bringing them to dramatic completion. In deft strokes the evangelists tell us of the final hours of Jesus' life—his last meal with his disciples, his arrest in Gethsemane, his interrogation by the religious leaders, the trial before Pilate, and finally the heart-clutching scenes of Jesus' crucifixion, death and burial.

The passion narratives are rooted in historical memories of the early church and certainly reflect much of the Jewish world that Jesus knew and loved. Unlike most of the gospel story, which is located in the northern region of Galilee where Jesus did most of his public ministry, the passion stories take place in Jerusalem, the capital of the southern province of Judea and, for most Jews since the time of King David in the ninth century B.C., the identifying center of Jewish life.

Here in Jerusalem was located the temple, the most sacred place in Israel where God's presence was most evident. The inner sanctuary of the temple had contained the Ark of the Covenant, the mobile shrine containing the tablets of the law that Israel carried on its desert trek from Egypt to the promised land. No one passed through the veil that shrouded this inner sanctuary and entered this absolute zone of the sacred, except the high priest who, once a year on the feast of Yom Kippur, the day of atonement, would enter to symbolically purify the sanctuary from any effects of sin that happened to have penetrated that holy place.

Assigned to the temple were the priests and Levites who maintained the temple liturgy and assisted the streams of pilgrims who would come from Israel and from all over the Mediterranean world to offer sacrifice and pray during the great pilgrimage feasts of the Jewish liturgical year. It was built by the master builder Herod the Great who left the heritage of his massive building projects all over Israel—the harbor city of Caesarea, the northern capital of Samaria, the fortified palaces of Masada and the Herodium—to name just a few. But the Jerusalem temple was his crown jewel, and this awe-inspiring structure with its massive walls, its exquisite decorations and its broad plazas was just in the final stages of its construction when Jesus came here to complete his mission sometime around the year A.D. 30.

Since the time of David, Jerusalem had also been a political center; the seat of the unified monarchy under David and Solomon and then of the southern kingdom of Judea in subsequent centuries. In Jesus' day, however, Jerusalem and the provinces of Judea and Samaria were under direct Roman rule, the only areas of Israel fated to be so. Archelaus, one of the sons of Herod the Great who had been designated by the Romans as a Jewish vassal king over this region after Herod's death, proved to be cruel and inept and was eventually deposed by the Romans in 6 A.D. Ever since, a string of Roman procurators had assumed direct rule of Judea and Samaria, using the coastal city of Caesarea Maritima as the seat of government and venturing to Jerusalem only for state visits, particularly during the great Jewish festivals when a tighter grip on the reins was called for. In 30 A.D., the current Roman procurator of Judea was Pontius Pilate and, according to custom, he would come to Jerusalem for the Jewish festival of Passover.

Thus the stage was set for the passion drama. Jesus, the Galilean prophet, healer and extraordinary teacher, would bring his mission to Jerusalem. A few days before the festival, surrounded by the devoted and curious, he had entered into the holy city and its gleaming temple. There, in the manner of a prophet, he had performed a series of dramatic and daring actions, disrupting the services that allowed pilgrims to exchange profane Roman coins for appropriate temple currency and blocking those who were entering to perform their devotions—gestures all apparently calculated as a prophetic statement that this temple, no matter how magnificent, would be swept away in the coming messianic age.

Jesus' reputation as a provocative teacher and awesome healer may have preceded him to Jerusalem. We do not know for sure, but certainly his action in the temple must have been seen as dangerous to both Jew and Roman alike. While the Romans held the reins of ultimate power in Judea, they counted on local Jewish authorities—the leading priests and other elders—to maintain public order. The religious leaders had no love for the Romans and were people devoted to freedom for Israel, but they, too, would be wary of anyone who might give the Romans an excuse for interference and further repression, especially one who, at the same time, seemed to be making provocative religious claims for himself and his mission.

The passion stories agree on some of the basic stages of Jesus' final days. He came to Jerusalem to celebrate with his disciples the feast of Passover, the yearly commemoration of Israel's liberation from slavery in Egypt and an affirmation of its hope for God's future deliverance. The night before his death, after a last meal with his disciples, he went with them to pray at an olive grove on the western slope of the Mount of Olives, facing the temple mount. There he was arrested by an armed band authorized by the religious leaders, and perhaps already with the backing of the Roman authorities as well. One of his own disciples, Judas Iscariot, had alerted the authorities to Jesus' whereabouts. Later that night Jesus was interrogated by a gathering of the religious authorities, probably in an attempt to formulate charges against him.

The next day he was brought before Pilate for a formal hearing, since Pilate, who was probably staying at Herod's former palace in the upper part of the city, had the official jurisdiction in such cases. After some hesitation, Pilate condemned Jesus to crucifixion, a terrible Roman form of public execution usually reserved for cases that involved sedition. Perhaps Pilate thought of Jesus as a slightly crazed, yet still potentially dangerous, pretendant to royal power.

Execution of the sentence was, as usual, swift. Jesus was flogged and then led in procession through the streets of the city to a mound reserved for public executions near a cemetery outside one of the city gates of Jerusalem. There he was stripped naked and then spiked to the cross. Crucifixion was a public event, meant to humiliate the victim through a slow and tortuous death and thereby discredit his cause. Jesus died after only a few hours on the cross, probably from asphyxiation. Someone sympathetic to Jesus who apparently owned a cave-like tomb in the nearby limestone cemetery requested permission to remove the body of Jesus from the cross and have him buried before sundown, in accord with Jewish custom.

These, then, are the stark basic "facts" of Jesus' final hours detectable in the passion stories. Yet these brute facts alone do not command the interest of the gospels. Far more important to the gospel writers was the significance of this story of suffering and death because of who it is that suffered. The passion narratives are not police blotters reporting the cold facts of a public execution, but are an essential part of the Christian story of Jesus, the Son of God, and his exultant triumph over death. The gospels are proclamation—preaching, if you will—telling in story form the meaning of Jesus' life, death and resurrection for us.

So from the very beginning of the church, Christians gathered not only to remember the story of Jesus' death but to understand that death in the light of his resurrection and against the backdrop of God's word, the Old Testament, the early church's Bible. In retelling the story of Jesus' death from the vantage point of resurrection faith, the early Christians hoped to understand more not only about Jesus but also more about the meaning of their own encounter with suffering and death.

The original passion story that would later influence Mark's own passion narrative probably first took shape in a setting of worship, not unlike the Holy Week Triduum when Christians gather each year to celebrate in prayer Jesus' last supper with his disciples, his passion and death and his triumphant resurrection. So, too, the earliest Christian communities would come together in a spirit of prayer and reflection, to recall the key events of those fateful days in Jerusalem but also to pray the psalms and meditate on the prophets and the great texts of their scriptures that gave meaning to those events. Over time, this blend of historical recital and accompanying prayers and biblical readings would blend together so that now they are inseparable in the passion accounts that have come down to us in the gospels.

When he took up the task of composing his gospel, the evangelist Mark must have had access to such a passion story, perhaps one handed down by memory and cherished in the worship of his own Christian community. As Mark told his story of Jesus' life, that passion story would form its endpoint and climax, a pattern that would be followed by each of the other gospels.

Our goal, therefore, is to read the passion stories in the spirit in which they were written, intent not so much on retrieving the history that stands behind these texts but rather to absorb the faith understanding of Jesus' death that suffuses them. Lost in the familiarity of these stories that most of us have heard all our lives, may be the fact that each evangelist tells the account of Jesus' suffering and death in a distinct way.

Because each evangelist wrote for a different Christian community and because each of them was gifted with a unique style of narration and a particular point of view, the four accounts are diverse. Like four great artists, each evangelist produced a masterful portrait of the crucified Jesus. This is true of their gospel stories as a whole and remains true for the way they present the passion of Jesus. We will savor each of their accounts in turn.

THE PASSION ACCORDING TO MARK

The Gospel of Mark was probably the first gospel to be written, so we will begin with his passion story. Like his gospel as a whole, Mark's passion narrative is lean and taut, moving swiftly and in a haunting fashion from the events of the last supper to Jesus' death and burial.

Fidelity and Betrayal: The Passion Begins (14:1-11)

Mark begins the passion with three stories of brooding, shameful betrayal and tender fidelity. The enemies of Jesus, often the Pharisees and now the Jerusalem based priests and elders, never step out of character in which the evangelist has portrayed them from the beginning of the gospel. They had hounded Jesus during his ministry in Galilee and intensified their opposition to his teaching when he had arrived in Jerusalem. Now their implacable hostility is sealed with a plot to take his life.

A chilling new element is added, however: Judas, one of Jesus' own disciples—chosen and loved and entrusted with a share in Jesus' mission—goes to the leaders and offers to betray Jesus to them. They are pleased and pay him for his service.

In between these stories, with a dramatic touch typical of his gospel, Mark inserts a story of exquisite fidelity. While Jesus visits Simon the Leper in Bethany on the eastern slopes of the Mount of Olives, an anonymous woman breaks open her alabaster jar of costly perfumed oil, and anoints Jesus' head. In the Bible, kings and prophets were anointed on the head, and Mark plays on that memory here.

As the fragrance of the oil fills the room, those with Jesus are shocked at the woman's extravagant gesture. But Jesus defends her. She performed an act of true fidelity and love, he tells them, "she has anticipated anointing my body for burial" (14:8). For this, Jesus promises, she would be remembered wherever the Gospel would be preached, the only one in all of the New Testament to be so greatly honored.

These three sharply contrasting scenes thrust the reader into the heart of Mark's message. Two major themes run through the entire passion story—one focusing on Jesus, who with intense determination gives his life for others; the other, on those who surround Jesus, some withering in the crucible of suffering, some exemplifying faith and courage.

The passion exposes the terrible intent of Judas and the leaders, but it also gives us a glimpse of authentic discipleship in the anonymous woman of Bethany. She, like Jesus, understands both who he is and what his destiny entails and without hesitation acts on that intuition. And therefore she anoints him for burial and acclaims his royal dignity. For such love she would never be forgotten.

The Final Passover (14:12-31)

Mark's Gospel is noted for its manner of framing a key scene with two other related stories. That takes place in the next

portion of the passion story: Jesus' words over the bread and wine are framed by his predictions of Judas' betrayal and Peter's and the rest of the disciples' failure. Once again Mark's dual focus on christology and discipleship—so characteristic of his gospel—is in evidence. Celebration of the Passover is the setting for all of these stories. Israel's great pilgrimage feast commemorated the exodus from Egypt, God's act of liberating love that was the basis of Israel's hope. So the gospel highlights the fact that Jesus' encounter with death, a death that would liberate others, was entwined with the Passover.

Mark uses the bare ritual of the Passover meal to proclaim in Jesus' own words the meaning of the passion. Jesus takes bread, gives thanks, breaks it, and gives it to his disciples, saying, "This is my body"; and then he takes a cup, once again offers thanks and gives it to the disciples, saying, "This is my blood of the covenant, which will be shed for many . . ." (14:22, 24).

Here was the inner meaning of every act of Jesus' ministry which Mark had narrated earlier in the gospel: Jesus' compassionate healing, his befriending of those left on the margins, his forceful teaching, his confrontations with evil, his feeding of the hungry crowds. All of this was a life given for the others, all of this was "bread broken" and "blood . . . shed for many." Such was the spirit of his mission that would ultimately end in triumph and such was the mission the disciples were called to carry out. But there was a long road ahead and much pain and conversion of heart before they would be ready. And so Jesus' solemn words and eloquent gestures at the sup-

per are framed with his predictions that Judas Iscariot would fail tragically and the rest of his disciples would abandon him. Even Simon Peter, the first disciple to be called (1:16-20) and their leader, would publicly disown Jesus out of fear and abandon his master.

Mark's Gospel never hesitates to underscore the cost of discipleship.

Gethsemane: Prayer and Arrest (14:32-52)

Now the setting shifts from the upper room to Gethsemane, an olive grove on the outskirts of the city, and here in two major scenes the pace of the passion story quickens.

The specter of violent death hovers over Jesus and torments him. As he had done several times in the gospel Jesus gathers his strength in prayer. It is not a polite or heroic prayer but one that echoes the raw expressions of faith found in the psalms: "Abba, Father, all things are possible to you. Take this cup away from me, but not what I will but what you will" (14:36). So much of the spirit of Jesus is here: his tenacious and intimate devotion to God, his "Abba," the fierce struggles with the power of evil and death that marked his ministry in Galilee (see, for example, 5:1-20).

Mark informs his readers early in the Gospel that Jesus is the Son of God, one in whom the Spirit abides and one whose name God speaks at the Jordan (1:9-11) and on the mount of Transfiguration (9:7). But Jesus is also genuinely human, wary of death and crushed by the thought that his mission was running aground. So Mark dares to present us with this scene, one that would be fixed in Christian memory forever: a wrenching prayer of faith and fear from the lips of Jesus.

Mark continues his method of presenting the disciples in stark counterpoint with Jesus. Three times he comes to find support in their presence, only to find them sleeping. The Gospel had already made clear that this "sleep" is not mere fatigue at the end of a long celebration. This brand of sleep could be deadly; it was the spiritual torpor of those who do not recognize the moment of crisis in history and do not prepare themselves to face it. Jesus had warned the disciples about this type of "sleep": "Watch, therefore; you do not know when the lord of the house is coming, whether in the evening, or at midnight, or at cockcrow, or in the morning. May he not come suddenly and find you sleeping. What I say to you, I say to all: 'Watch!' " (13:35-37).

That moment of crisis comes swiftly. Judas and an armed crowd break into the stillness of Gethsemane to arrest Jesus, the apostate disciple identifying Jesus with a treacherous kiss. Mayhem breaks out: they seize Jesus and arrest him; meanwhile a "bystander" (one of the crowd? one of Jesus' followers?) lashes out with a sword and wounds a servant of the High Priest.

Jesus faces that wall of violence and condemns it: "Have you come out as against a robber, with swords and clubs, to seize me? Day after day I was with you teaching in the temple area, yet you did not arrest me; but that the scriptures may be fulfilled" (14:48-49). How often has this scene been repeated in the centuries since Mark wrote: a nighttime arrest; the forces of violence seeking to destroy the voice of justice; violence breeding more violence; the lone heroic stance of the martyr who refuses to betray the spirit of God.

Again Mark contrasts the response of the disciples with that of Jesus. The crisis has come, and they cannot endure it. All of them flee, abandoning Jesus, one of them so panic stricken that he tears away from the grip of his captor and flees naked. The disciples have left behind their dignity, their calling, and the one who gave them life.

Jesus before the Sanhedrin (14:53-72)

The scene shifts once more: from Gethsemane to the residence of the High Priest where Jesus will be interrogated by the leaders. Mark's masterful narrative style is again in evidence. He frames the interrogation scene with that of Peter's denials, clearly contrasting the disciple's fear with Jesus' courage.

A parade of false witnesses are brought forward against Jesus, but their accusations are contradictory. Some, however, bring up a charge that jogs the memory of the reader of the Gospel: "I will destroy this temple made with hands and within three days I will build another not made with hands." Earlier in the gospel, Mark had presented Jesus as a prophet on fire with zeal, purging the temple and predicting its demise (11:15-19; 13:1-2). Indeed the Risen Christ would be the new temple of God, the "rejected stone" that would become the cornerstone of a new sacred people in whom God would dwell (12:10-11). This accusation of the trial would be remembered when the veil of the sanctuary would tear apart at the moment of Jesus' death (15:38).

Frustrated by the flawed testimony of his witnesses, the High Priest poses the key question to Jesus: "Are you the Messiah, the Son of the Blessed One?" There is no hesitation in Jesus' reply: "I am." And he adds a challenge to his opponents: they would one day see their prisoner coming as the "Son of Man," that haunting figure who would experience humiliation and rejection, but then would be lifted up in exaltation by God and return in triumph at the end of the world.

Jesus' bold declaration of his identity is rejected as blasphemous by his opponents; they condemn him to death and begin to abuse him. The reader who knows who Jesus truly is can only marvel in deep sadness at how spiritually blind we are all capable of becoming.

Mark shifts our attention from Jesus standing before his captors back to the courtyard below, where Peter warily edges near a group of servants huddling around a warm fire. As if in slow motion, we watch the power of fear break down a disciple's resolve. Three times Peter denies he even knows Jesus, finally cursing and swearing as panic takes hold. A cock crows and Peter remembers Jesus' warning at the supper. The terrible realization of his failure surges over him, and he begins to weep.

The story is so familiar that we may not be able to recapture its incredible shock. The full measure of the disciples' failure can be taken in this single tragic story: the leader of those whom Jesus called publicly to discipleship renounces his allegiance to his Master.

The Roman Trial
(15:1-21)

The leaders take Jesus to Pilate to have him condemned to crucifixion. Mark rivets our attention on a single issue— Jesus' identity as king—as for the first time the power of Rome enters the passion story.

The scene is full of irony. Pilate, the representative of imperial power, confronts this battered Jewish prisoner and questions him on his supposed pretensions to be "king of the Jews." While Jesus' own people reject their true king and choose Barabbas, a murderer, Pilate, a Gentile and a Roman, appears convinced of Jesus' innocence and seeks to have him released.

Underneath all of this is the issue of kingship, the most forceful expression of human political power known to Mark's readers. Pilate and Jesus' opponents agree on one thing: Jesus is no king. In Pilate's mind he is a harmless victim of the leaders' envy; to the leaders he is a false and dangerous claimant to religious authority. So ultimately Jesus is mocked for his pretensions to kingship: a cloak of purple, a crown of thorns, a reed scepter, and a parody of homage that turns violent.

However, the reader of Mark's passion story knows that it is not Jesus but those symbols of imperial and abusive power that are being mocked. Jesus is a king but one whose power is expressed not in exploiting or "lording it over others" (10:42) but in giving them life. Earlier in the gospel during the journey to Jerusalem, Jesus had urged his disciples not to exercise that kind of power but only the power whose source and intent is to give life to others, the very power that animated Jesus himself (10:42-45). The passion story, therefore, stands in judgment over all forms of abusive power.

Crucifixion (15:22-47)

The end comes swiftly in Mark's account; the story is told in few words, as if it were too painful to say more. Pilate gives up his attempts to free Jesus and condemns him to crucifixion. An execution detail brings Jesus to Golgotha, where he is offered a narcotic (which he refuses), stripped of his garments and nailed to the cross. Two rebels are crucified with Jesus one on each side of him, forming a sad entourage. The sign over the cross acclaims in derision: "The King of the Jews."

During the death watch, a parade of mockery dredges up the issues of the trial and hurls them at the man on the cross: his threats to the temple; his power to save others and now his inability to save himself. Mark casts this last taunt in strongly ironic tones: "Let the Messiah, the King of Israel, come down now from the cross that we may see and believe" (15:32). But the reader knows that Jesus' power is demonstrated not in shedding the cross but in carrying it, in giving his life for others. "Whoever wishes to come after me must deny themselves, take up the cross, and follow me. For whoever wishes to save their life will lose it, but whoever loses their life for my sake and that of the gospel will save it" (8:34-37).

Darkness envelopes Golgotha and out of that darkness comes Jesus' final lament: "My God, my God, why have you forsaken me?" It is the first verse of Psalm 22, the great Jewish prayer of suffering faith. Mark's passion story has been described as a "dark passage"— Jesus stripped of his disciples, his freedom, his dignity, his life as he gives every fiber of his being for the sake of the world. And so in Mark's account, Jesus dies with a wordless scream that echoes from that dread hill, splitting the veil of the temple and igniting faith in the centurion's heart. This unlikely witness sees in the manner of Jesus' death for others the true revelation of God. The sight of the Crucified Jesus triggers in him the full first confession of faith expressed in the gospel: "Truly this man was the Son of God!" (15:39). A startling revelation—God's power revealed not through staggering prodigies but in a selfless death motivated by love.

Mark has an eye for the unlikely. The chosen disciples had long fled. But standing at a distance were other faithful followers, the women who had been drawn to Jesus in Galilee and had come to Jerusalem with him. They would stay with him now through death and burial, never abandoning him. Two of them, Mary Magdalene and Mary the mother of Joses, would keep vigil at his burial and would be the first to discover the tomb empty and to know that Jesus was victorious over death (16:1-8). These "unlikely disciples," who proved true where others more prominent had failed, would be the ones to bring the Risen Christ's message of joy and reconciliation to the disciples who had failed.

Now the Easter story could begin.

THE PASSION ACCORDING TO MATTHEW

Throughout his gospel, Matthew follows closely the storyline of his primary source Mark but still colors that story with themes characteristic of his gospel. The same is true of the passion story where Matthew's account absorbs virtually all of Mark's story; yet here, too, Matthew recasts the narrative to highlight his own distinctive themes. In meeting death Jesus fulfills his God-given destiny foreshadowed in the Scriptures and inaugurates a new age of history charged with resurrection life. Jesus is the obedient Son of God, tenaciously faithful even in the midst of abject suffering. Jesus' trust in God, tested in the savage fury of death itself, is not in vain.

The Gathering Storm (26:1-16)

Matthew portrays Jesus' passion as an encounter with destiny, not a destiny of blind fate but one made inevitable by the strong commitments of Jesus' mission from God and the fierce resistance of the power of death.

The opening scenes of the passion story set the mood. Matthew begins with a solemn introduction (26:1-5): now that Jesus has finished all of his life-giving words to Israel, he is ready to enact his most powerful teaching and most compelling example. With the penetrating insight of the Son of God, Jesus calmly foretells to his disciples the coming events of the passion.

In contrast with the serenity of Jesus, the religious leaders gather to forge a desperate plot. Even as they determine to arrest him "by treachery" they fear Jesus' magnetic hold on the people of Israel. Throughout his gospel Matthew portrays the religious leaders in a single, negative dimension. They symbolize opposition to Jesus, and his message and their vices illustrate what a disciple is not to be.

Not everyone rejected Jesus, as the poignant scene of the anointing demonstrates (26:6-13). When he is in Bethany on the outskirts of Jerusalem dining in Simon the leper's home (so typical of Jesus' compassion for the sick and outcasts), an unnamed woman offers Jesus a lavish gesture of hospitality and love. She anoints his head with precious perfumed oil.

While in the first-century world anointing guests with oil was not unknown in banquets of the wealthy, the disciples of Jesus consider the woman's action as shocking and extravagant. But for Jesus and the gospel, this act of lavish love is just right for the fateful moment of the passion. The woman anoints Jesus on the head, just as prophets and kings were anointed—thus she offers Jesus the homage he is due. And, as Jesus himself proclaims, in lovingly anointing his body she has prepared him for death and burial. Loving reverence for Jesus and an understanding of his death are signs of true discipleship—and so the bold gesture of this anonymous woman would be remembered "wherever this gospel is proclaimed in the whole world." Without question, this is the most remarkable endorsement of any character in the entire New Testament.

In stark contrast to the tender and bold love of the woman, Judas, one of

Jesus' twelve apostles, goes to the chief priests and sells his soul in betraying Jesus. Matthew alone notes the counting out of "thirty pieces of silver," the price of a slave according to Exodus 21:32. Undoubtedly, Judas was a painful enigma to the early community: how could one of the Twelve chosen by Jesus so betray him? Matthew's Gospel does not underestimate the corrosive influence of money and greed: "Where your heart is, there will your treasure be. . . . You cannot serve God and mammon" (6:21, 24).

The cast of characters is on stage—Jesus, his disciples, his opponents. The machinery of betrayal and death begins to turn. And, notes Matthew, Judas went out looking "for an opportunity to hand him over" (26:16). The Greek word Matthew uses for "opportunity" is *eukairian*—the *kairos*, the moment of choice and destiny. There is irony here: Both Judas and Jesus move towards the same fateful moment—for one it will be a time of betrayal and self-destruction; for Jesus, a moment of ultimate fidelity and life-giving.

**The Kairos
(26:17-35)**

The next set of scenes focus on Jesus' last meal with his disciples. It is the eve of Passover, the beginning of the great pilgrimage feast when Jews from all over Israel and across the Roman world celebrated the Exodus, God's liberation of the people from slavery and death. With majestic solemnity Jesus begins the preparation for his last Passover. He sends disciples into Jerusalem giving them precise instructions on preparing for the supper. The words of Jesus,

unique to Matthew, are filled with meaning: "My appointed time draws near" (26:18). The Greek word *kairos* is used again, signifying the decisive moment of history when an old world would die and a new age would be born. For Matthew the death and resurrection of Jesus are in fact the turning point in all of human destiny.

The disciples obediently follow Jesus' commands and all is ready for the Passover celebration. The mood of this farewell supper is laced with both sadness and exultation. In Semitic culture as in so many others, the meal was a sacred moment, a time in which the common bonds of life and friendship were to be celebrated. Against that backdrop, Jesus predicts that one of the twelve would violate the bond between disciple and master. The other disciples are distressed and ask the question that is to echo in the heart of every Christian who has to face his or her infidelity: "Surely it is not I, Lord?" (26:22).

Judas becomes the antitype of the disciple, a figure that seems to fascinate the evangelist. All of human history is entwined mysteriously with God's providence, even the terrible failure of apostasy and betrayal. But the reality of God's providential love does not rob us of our responsibility. Throughout his gospel Matthew lingers over this theme: we are accountable to God for our choices and our actions. If Judas chooses death, death he will experience. As if sealing his fate, Judas echoes the question of the other disciples: "Surely it is not I, Rabbi?" (26:25), an ironic touch found only in Matthew's account.

At the conclusion of the meal Jesus would return to the tragic theme of betrayal and failure (26:31-34). Not only Judas but all of the disciples, including Peter, whom Jesus had blessed as their leader (16:16) and sustained upon the chaotic sea (14:28-31), would find their loyalty to Jesus break upon the shoals of intense suffering and fear. Even these bleakest of moments do not escape the embrace of God's Word; the failure of the disciples fulfills the prophecy of Zechariah 13:7, "I will strike the shepherd, and the sheep of the flock will be dispersed."

These predictions of betrayal and failure form a poignant frame around the key moment of the Passover meal. Using vivid, indelible symbols, Jesus tells the disciples the meaning of his death. The bread broken is his body given for them; the cup poured out is his blood, the "blood of the covenant" offering God's forgiveness and unquenchable love to all. All of Jesus' ministry—every word of liberating truth, every healing touch, every confrontation with injustice—is distilled here in the bread and the cup, in the body and blood of Jesus given totally for the sake of the world.

This last supper is not really the final Passover for Jesus and his disciples. He would celebrate it again "new" in the Kingdom of God. Despite their weakness Jesus' fiercely loyal love for the disciples would gather them once again beyond the boundaries of death.

Gethsemane (26:36-56)

The pace of the passion story begins to quicken. Jesus and his disciples leave the supper room and go to a secluded grove of olive trees (Luke locates Gethsemane on the Mount of Olives). There Jesus takes three of his disciples and begins a vigil of intense and anguished prayer. His words evoke Psalm 42—"My soul is sorrowful even to death" (26:38). The master who had taught his disciples the importance of direct, honest and trusting prayer (6:5-15) now prays with all his heart as he looks into the face of death. Jesus falls prostrate on the ground and opens his spirit to God: "My Father, if it is possible, let this cup pass from me; yet, not as I will, but as you will" (26:39).

All of the mystery of Jesus is expressed in this prayer: a human being clinging to life and fearing death; a faithful child of God who places all of his future in the hands of a loving Father.

Three times Jesus repeats his intense prayer. He had asked his disciples to keep vigil with him, but they are overwhelmed with sleep and once more fail their master. Their sleep is symbolic of their spiritual torpor—they are not prepared for the fury of death that is about to sweep through Gethsemane and threaten the life of Jesus.

The storm of death arrives when Judas leads a large crowd armed with swords and clubs into the garden to arrest Jesus (26:47). Once again Matthew's Gospel gives special attention to this doomed disciple. With scorching irony a kiss becomes the sign of treachery. As he had at the supper, Judas masks his betrayal with seemingly innocent words: "Hail, Rabbi!" But Jesus sees deeply into the soul of Judas and even in the very instant of betrayal addresses him as "Friend."

The armed mob takes Jesus captive, but in a futile gesture one of the disciples draws a sword and severs the ear of the high priest's servant. In Matthew's account this becomes an opportunity for Jesus to teach. He warns the disciple not to return violence for violence—those who live by the sword die by the sword. In the Sermon on the Mount, Jesus had urged his disciples not to turn to violence (5:21-26, 38-42); a child of God must love even the enemy (5:43-48). If it were a simple matter of displays of power, God could overwhelm Jesus' attackers with legions of angels. But God's reign revealed in the Scriptures would not be imposed by violence. Jesus' fidelity would take him into the valley of death but, ultimately, the Scriptures would be fulfilled and love would defeat violence and death.

But for now the forces of evil seem to have the upper hand. Faced with that prospect, the disciples succumb to fear and desert Jesus to his captors.

Jesus on Trial
(26:57—27:10)

The mob leads its prisoner to Caiaphas the high priest and the assembled scribes and elders. Matthew portrays this as a formal hearing in which the leaders listen to testimony against Jesus, interrogate him and finally condemn him.

The gospel's dramatic sense is evident. The whole scene of Jesus on trial, fearlessly facing his captors, is framed by the story of Peter's denial. While the other disciples had fled in headlong panic, Peter had trailed the mob at a distance and followed his captive master into the courtyard of the high priest. But here his ebbing courage would fail him. Some of the maidservants recognize him as a companion of Jesus the Galilean; under this scrutiny Peter denies his discipleship, swearing with an oath that "I do not know the man!" Jesus had warned his disciples to avoid oaths and to tell the plain truth (5:33-37); now Peter compounds his failures. At that moment the cock crows, and the broken disciple remembers Jesus' warning at the supper. The enormity of his failure crashing in on him, Peter leaves the courtyard and weeps bitterly.

Jesus meanwhile stands before the high priest and the Sanhedrin. The parade of witnesses against Jesus is not impressive, so finally the high priest must confront the silent captive: "I order you to tell us under oath before the living God whether you are the Messiah, the Son of God" (26:63). The reader who has followed Jesus through the gospel knows the answer to this question: Jesus, born in the Spirit; Jesus the revealer of God's truth and bearer of God's healing power—this man is, indeed, the longed-for Messiah and God's unique Son.

The high priest's own phrasing states the truth he cannot recognize. Jesus goes on to prophesy that he will be exalted as the triumphant Son of Man enthroned at God's right hand and coming at the end of time on the clouds of heaven (26:64). But for now such triumph is apparent only to the eye of faith; for the leaders this man is no Messiah but an impostor and blasphemer worthy of death. Their hostility spills over into violence and mockery as they spit on Jesus and strike him, taunting his claims to messianic power (26:67). At dawn the assembly reconvenes, and they formally condemn Jesus to death and lead him away to Pilate, the Roman governor.

Before Matthew concludes this scene he picks up the thread of Judas's story (27:3-10). The betrayer is overwhelmed with regret and attempts to return the thirty pieces of silver to the religious leaders, confessing that he has betrayed innocent blood.

But they rebuff him and in despair he casts the coins into the temple and takes his own life. Even though the leaders had refused the blood money it still comes back to haunt them. They collect the coins and use them to purchase a burial plot for strangers.

This tragic story strangely echoes for Matthew the foreboding story of Jeremiah 19, where the prophet breaks a potter's flask in a field as a sign of judgment on Jerusalem, a field that would be used to bury strangers. Once again for Matthew's Gospel even the most abject moments of human existence do not fall outside of God's encompassing purpose.

The Messiah Condemned (27:11-32)

The passion story shifts to a new scene as Jesus is brought to trial before Pilate, the Roman procurator. Now themes of kingship and allegiance come to the fore.

Pilate questions Jesus on his identity as a king, but the mysterious prisoner offers no response to the accusations hurled at him by the leaders. The Christian reader knows that Jesus is truly a king but a king unlike any that Pilate could understand.

It was apparently a custom to release to the crowd a prisoner of their choice on the occasion of the Passover. Pilate offers the assembled people a choice of either Barabbas, a "notorious prisoner" (27:16) or Jesus. Ancient manuscripts suggest that Matthew may have dramatically heightened the focus of the choice by having Barabbas actually named "Jesus the one called Barabbas" paralleling "Jesus, the one called the Christ."

Each time Pilate offers that choice the leaders and the crowds choose to free Barabbas and demand to have Jesus crucified. Matthew builds the drama to the final moment. In a gesture reminiscent of the ritual for declaring innocence in Deuteronomy 21, Pilate washes his hands and tells the crowd: "I am innocent of this man's blood. Look to it yourselves." In reply, the "whole people" declares: "His blood be upon us and upon our children" (27:24-25).

For nearly two thousand years, this passage has been tragically misinterpreted as an excuse to punish Jews for their supposed guilt for the death of Jesus. There is no question that Matthew intends this as a dramatic and decisive moment. Jesus, Son of Abraham, Son of David, had come to his people and like the prophets before him had experienced rejection. All of the opposition led by the errant leaders now culminates here in the passion story. While the Gentile Pilate declares his innocence, Jesus' own people accept responsibility for his innocent blood. Matthew sees here a turning point in history which would ultimately lead to the mission to the Gentiles.

But did the evangelist intend this text as a perpetual condemnation of his own Jewish people? Certainly not! Matthew surely faulted Jesus' contemporaries for not being open to the gospel and may even have interpreted the destruction of the Temple and Jerusalem during the Jewish revolt of 66-70 A.D. as a sign of God's punishment on that generation (that is, "us and our children"). But there is no evidence he intended this text to be an excuse for anti-Semitism, or believed that Jesus' own Jewish people should be exempt from being treated with the same compassion, forgiveness and justice the disciples of Jesus should show to every human being, and how much more the very flesh and blood to which Jesus belongs.

Jesus the king was now condemned by his own people and by the Roman authorities. The soldiers mock his seeming powerlessness, using the symbols of imperial power—the crown, the scepter, and the rituals of homage—to deride Jesus. But the reader knows another truth: Jesus is invested with God's power—not the oppressive power of brute force or domination but the liberating power of love and justice.

The Dawn of the New Age (27:33-66)

The climax of Matthew's passion narrative is filled with drama. His cross carried by Simon the Cyrenian, Jesus is led to Golgotha for crucifixion. The executioners affix a placard to the cross: "This is Jesus: the King of the Jews." They obviously intend the words to ridicule this messianic pretender as he is defeated in death. Similarly, a stream of passersby mock Jesus' claims to authority over the temple and taunt him by reminding him that he could apparently save others but not save himself. Even the two rebels crucified with him join in the chorus of revulsion.

In describing this terrible moment, Matthew once again reaches back to the Hebrew scriptures for his inspiration. As in Mark's gospel, Jesus' final prayer will be taken from Psalm 22, the great prayer of lament. In that powerful text, a faithful Jew prays in the midst of abject suffering and isolation. He is surrounded by people who ridicule his trust in God. Feeling abandoned even by God, the psalmist utters a prayer of raw faith: "My God, my God, why have you forsaken me?" It is that honest, unadorned prayer that Matthew places on the lips of Jesus as the sky darkens; God's faithful Son encounters death.

But just as the lament psalm turns unexpectedly to a hymn of triumph and praise (see Psalm 22:23-32), the crucifixion scene is transformed into an explosion of triumph. It is as if God responds to the lingering sound of Jesus' death prayer: the veil of the Temple is torn in half, the earth shakes, the rocks split and the tombs are opened. In a triumphant procession the saints who had been trapped in death enter the holy city of Jerusalem. The Roman soldiers who had kept the death watch over Jesus are astounded and acclaim Jesus as the true Son of God.

Matthew's Gospel anticipates in this triumphant scene the glory of the resurrection. Evoking Ezekiel's great vision of the dry bones (see Ezekiel 37:1-14), the evangelist proclaims that God has responded to the obedient death of Jesus by raising him and all the saints of Israel from death to new life. Earthquakes, the raising of the dead—these were all biblical signs of the end of the world. And in a very true sense, Jesus' death marked the end of a world without hope and the beginning of a new age of God's Spirit.

Still to come in the gospel story was the reverent burial by Joseph, the futile attempts of Jesus' opponents to contain him even in death, and the visit of the faithful women disciples to the tomb to anoint Jesus' body. But in Matthew's Gospel these are almost anti-climactic because resurrection breaks out on Golgotha itself, at the very moment death seems to have the upper hand. The trust of Jesus even in the face of mockery and abandonment is met immediately by God's abundant life and immortal embrace.

THE PASSION ACCORDING TO LUKE

One of the dominant images of Jesus in the Gospel of Luke is that of Jesus as the Spirit-filled prophet. Luke begins Jesus' public ministry in his hometown synagogue of Nazareth, opening the scroll to do the reading from the text of Isaiah 61, "The Spirit of the Lord is upon me because he has anointed me to bring glad tidings to the poor . . ." (Lk 4:16-30). That prophetic fire would drive Jesus throughout his ministry and bring him to the climax of his mission in Jerusalem. Therefore, it is not surprising that in Luke's Gospel Jesus faces his crucifixion with the courageous fidelity and prophetic sense of justice that had characterized his ministry all during the long journey from Galilee to Jerusalem.

The Last Supper (22:1-38)

Luke's Gospel delights in portraying Jesus at meals: the supper in the house of Simon the Pharisee where the woman had anointed Jesus and washed his feet with her tears and dried them with her hair, and in turn received the gift of unconditional forgiveness (7:36-50); meals with sinners that provoked the ire of his opponents (15:1-2); breaking bread with the crowds who hungered for his word (9:10-17).

This eloquent sign of Jesus' mission—the gathering of one people, breaking one bread—dominates the opening scenes of Luke's passion narrative. This meal would be the Passover (22:1, 7), the great liberation feast of Israel. On this very night Jesus' enemies had set a trap for him with the help of Judas, one of Jesus' own disciples (22:1-6). But Luke makes it clear that a drama more fateful than human failure is at work here: Satan, the prince of evil, "enters into Judas" and will attempt through such human agency to strike once more at the author of life (22:3). Once the preparations for the feast are completed, Jesus takes his place at table with the disciples. Jesus had longed to celebrate this festival with disciples; even more urgently he had longed for God's liberation of Israel, the meaning of this feast, and every fiber of his being was dedicated to that end.

The bread and the wine become signs of Jesus' own mission: his body broken and given, for them; his blood poured out in a new covenant, for them.

But the disciples do not yet fully comprehend who Jesus is or what is at stake on this Passover eve. Jesus warns them of impending betrayal but this seems only to confuse them. Even more poignant, nearly comic, is a scene unique to Luke's passion story. At this most solemn moment, the disciples begin to argue about which of them is the greatest (22:24). Jesus cuts through their clumsy arrogance by reaffirming the spirit of his own ministry: "I am among you as the one who serves" (22:27). The death of Jesus itself was the final act of service, the ultimate gift of life on behalf of others. This spirit was to characterize all expressions of authority and power in the Christian community. Luke's scene is perhaps overlooked in the Christian liturgy of Holy Week, but it has an impact no less compelling than the footwashing scene of John's passion story that we remember each Holy Thursday.

Luke's Gospel reserves a special role for the Twelve, that core group of Jesus' disciples. The very number was symbolic of the gathering of the lost tribes of Israel, the renewal of God's people that was the object of Jesus' mission. His disciples were to be the witnesses to Jesus' teaching and healing (24:44-49); they were to gather the church and take its mission to the ends of the earth (Acts 1:8). So Jesus prays for Simon and for the other disciples that the power of evil would not sweep them away (22:31-32). Even though Peter will weaken, the power of grace will draw him back, and his ministry, in turn, is to strengthen his brothers and sisters in the community. As we will see, the evangelist does his best to tell the passion story in this spirit, downplaying the impact of Peter's denial and passing over in silence the flight of the other disciples. For Luke the sure reconciliation that the Risen Christ brings to the community dissolves memories of its infidelities.

The Passover feast concludes with a strong warning from Jesus about the crisis that is soon to break upon this fragile community of disciples. They should "arm" themselves and be ready; Luke's Gospel does not underestimate, much less ignore, the aggressive power of evil that lifts its fist against the spirit of the gospel (22:35-38).

The Hour of Darkness (22:39-65)

The sense of crisis and danger that Luke injects into the passion story is apparent here in the haunting scenes of Jesus' anguished prayer, his nighttime arrest and interrogation. After the Passover feast, Jesus and his disciples go "to the Mount of Olives" (22:39). Luke situates this dramatic prayer of Jesus on that mountain where Judaism expected the end of the world to take place. And Luke alone describes Jesus' prayer as an "agony," one that causes him to perspire so that his sweat becomes as drops of blood. Greek literature used the term *agonia* to describe the extreme exertion of an athlete in training. So intense and anguished is Jesus' prayer as he prepares to encounter death that an "angel from heaven" comes to Jesus to strengthen him.

Jesus asks his disciples to join him in prayer that they, too, "would not undergo the test" (22:40). The "test" here means that final struggle between good and evil that Judaism expected at the end of the world, a "test" experienced whenever a person of faith encounters the aggressive power of death and evil in the world. Jesus' own prayer has that same fierce intensity: he is dedicated to doing his Father's will, but he also prays for deliverance from the power of death.

The very act of prayer, of pouring out one's anguish and fear before God, brings strength. So Jesus stands up and goes to find his disciples sleeping— "from grief" the evangelist notes, softening the impact of yet another sign of their weakness. Once again Jesus warns them of the approaching "test"; the community may not be ready for the fierce power of death but Jesus, the Son of God, is.

At that moment Judas brings a crowd to arrest Jesus. In Luke's account, his treacherous kiss never reaches Jesus because the Servant-Master already knows its purpose: "Judas, are you betraying the Son of Man with a kiss?" (22:48). The disciples, dazed by this onslaught and still not comprehending Jesus' teaching, reach for their weapons: "Lord, shall we strike with a sword?" (22:48). It is a question that Christians have often asked when confronted with evil. Without waiting for a reply, one disciple (unlike John, Luke does not identify him as Peter) slashes off the ear of the High Priest's servant. Characteristic of this gospel, Jesus' response to the issue of violent reprisal is to reach out and heal the wounded man. Jesus, who taught his disciples to "love your enemy" and not to return evil for evil (6:27-36), lives by his own words.

"This is your hour," Jesus tells the armed crowd, "the time for the power of darkness" (22:53). But the reader knows that beyond this nighttime, the resurrection day will come.

The scene shifts. Those arresting Jesus bring him to the house of the high priest (22:54-65). Here he will be interrogated and beaten throughout the night (22:63-65). These scenes of a furtive and violent arrest, of nighttime torture and interrogation have been repeated over and over in the history of Christian martyrdom, including our day.

Peter had followed his Master to the courtyard of the high priest's house and mingled with the crowd around a fire built to cheat the cold night air (22:54-62). But Peter's attempt to merge with the crowd fails; a maid recognizes him in the light of the fire: "This man too was with him." Fear rising in his throat, Peter vigorously denies that he even knows Jesus. But a little later the danger comes again as another person recognizes him, then "an hour later," another who catches Peter's Galilean accent. Each

time Peter—the leader of the twelve—denies that he ever heard of Jesus.

The first readers of this gospel, for whom Peter was still a fresh memory and the ancestor of their faith, must have found this scene painful. Luke adds a touch of exquisite drama and deep compassion. Unlike the other passion stories, the evangelist has staged this scene so that Peter and Jesus are within sight of each other: the warming fire and the knot of soldiers torturing Jesus are in the same courtyard. As the cock crows, the very signal that Jesus had foretold to Peter (22:34), Jesus turns and looks at his disciple. That gaze penetrates Peter's heart; he remembers Jesus' words, words warning of failure but also promising forgiveness, and leaves the courtyard weeping in remorse.

Jesus on Trial (22:66—23:25)

The long nighttime ends with an early morning session before the Sanhedrin, the ruling council of the Jews in Jerusalem. Although the gospel accounts give this event the semblance of a "trial," it was probably an informal hearing as the leaders prepared their case against Jesus for presentation before the Roman governor. Luke brings us quickly to the heart of the issue: the reader of this gospel knows from the opening scenes of the infancy narrative that Jesus is the "Messiah" and the "Son of God." But the opponents are closed to this truth.

The leaders bring Jesus to Pilate and begin to charge him with serious crimes. Luke alone emphasizes the political nature of the charges against Jesus: "We found this man misleading our people; he opposes the payment of taxes to Caesar and maintains that he is the Messiah, a king" (23:2). Later they repeat the charges: "He is inciting the people with his teaching throughout all Judea, from Galilee where he began even to here" (23:5).

Luke's account is filled with irony. It is ironic that the leaders whose responsibility was to defend the freedom and faith of Israel would become concerned with the rights of Caesar. But the reader of the gospel is aware of another level of irony: in fact, Jesus' powerful ministry of justice was a profound threat to the oppressive might of Caesar. And indeed his mission had intended to "stir up the people" as the Lucan Jesus has journeyed majestically from Galilee to Jerusalem. However, the revolution Jesus incited was not the predictable clash of alternate political systems, but a call for fundamental conversion and a vision of a renewed human family built on justice and compassion—a vision capable of shaking the foundation of every oppressive political system.

Further irony is found in the fact that the secular authorities, Pilate and then Herod, find Jesus innocent while the religious leaders tenaciously seek to destroy him. Luke has the Roman Governor and the vassal king of Galilee repeatedly affirm this. "I find this man not guilty," Pilate declares (23:4). And in a curious scene unique to Luke (23:6-16), even when Jesus is mocked as a bogus prophet by Herod Antipas, the corrupt king and murderer of prophets (9:7-9; 13:31-33) could find no guilt in Jesus.

So once again Pilate refuses to condemn Jesus; the charges of sedition are emphatically denied: "I have conducted my investigation in your presence and have not found this man guilty of the charges you have brought against him . . . so no capital crime has been committed by him" (23:14; see also 23:22).

Some biblical scholars think that in so doing, Luke wanted to assure his Roman readers that Jesus was not a political revolutionary and that the Christians could live in peace in the empire. Perhaps so, but Luke also presents Pilate (and even more so Herod) as weak and ultimately corrupt because he finally accedes to the demands of the leaders that Jesus be crucified. Rather than attempting to soothe the anxieties of Roman officials, it is more likely that Luke wanted to show that Jesus died unjustly yet without swerving from his fidelity to God's will. This had been the fate of the persecuted prophets of Israel, and it would be the fate of courageous followers of Jesus down to our own day. Jesus was the first Christian martyr, following the pattern of many of his Jewish ancestors who had suffered for their fidelity to God.

The Way of the Cross (23:26-32)

The devotion of the way of the cross finds its roots in Luke's passion story. He alone gives details about events along that final stretch of Jesus' journey from Galilee. The Messiah who has "set his face toward Jerusalem" (Luke 9:51) would now come to the summit of his journey to God.

As the execution detail leads Jesus from the Governor's palace to the rock quarry outside the gates of the city where public executions took place, they impound Simon of Cyrene, a passerby, to carry the cross of Jesus. Luke's wording makes it clear that he sees in the figure of Simon an image of discipleship: Simon takes up the cross of Jesus and carries it "behind Jesus." The phrase is identical to Jesus' own teaching on discipleship: "Whoever does not carry his own cross and come after me cannot be my disciple" (Lk 14:27). Those who would live the way of Jesus must be willing to pour out their life on behalf of others.

The sense of urgent crisis reasserts itself in Luke's story. The Jerusalem crowds are not all hostile to Jesus. Even though some joined in condemning him there are others who lament this tragedy (23:27). As the prophets had before him, Jesus warns the people of Jerusalem that sin has its consequences. Tears were not needed for Jesus but for the havoc that evil would bring upon the people of the Holy City. Luke's Gospel has ambivalent feelings about Jerusalem. From one point of view, it was the city of God, the locus of the temple where Jesus began his life and where the early community would gather in prayer after the resurrection. "From Jerusalem" the gospel would stream out into the world. But Jerusalem was also the murderer of the prophets and the symbol of rejection. Luke and the early church interpreted the terrible suffering that befell Jerusalem during the revolt against Rome in A.D.70 as a sign of sin's ultimate effect.

Luke adds one final, poignant detail to his description of Jesus' journey to the cross; with him march two criminals. The Jesus who had been described by his opponents as a "friend of tax collectors and sinners" (Lk 7:34) would not only live with such friends but die with them.

The Death of the Just Man (23:33-49)

Luke fills the crucifixion scene with details typical of his portrayal of Jesus. He is crucified with the two criminals surrounding him, fulfilling Jesus' own prediction at the supper table: "For I tell you that the scripture must be fulfilled in me, namely, 'He was counted among the wicked' " (22:37). Just as Jesus had repeatedly taught his disciples not to respond to violence with more violence and to be forgiving (6:27-36), so he forgives the very men who had condemned him and who drive the stakes into his body (23:34).

When one of the crucified criminals joins in the chorus of derision that accompanies Jesus to his death, the other confesses his sin and asks for mercy (23:39-43). It is Luke's prescription for authentic conversion as exemplified in the story of the publican and the sinner (18:9-14) and so Jesus promises this man not only forgiveness but a place at his side that very day as his journey to God triumphantly reaches its home in paradise.

The moment of Jesus' death is charged with drama. As a sign of the terrible power of death, the sun's light is eclipsed and darkness grips "the whole land" (23:44). The Temple veil covering the entrance to the Holy of Holies is torn in two—as if to say that even God's presence leaves the people. This is, indeed, the "hour of darkness."

From the midst of these terrible omens comes Jesus' piercing voice, his life breath poured out in a final prayer: "Father, into your hands I commend my spirit" (23:46). The words are from Psalm 31 (verse 6) and express the core of Jesus' being—his unshakable trust in God, a trust that death itself could not destroy.

His death has an immediate impact. The Roman centurion who had overseen his execution is struck to the heart by the manner of Jesus' death, the first of an endless stream of believers touched by the cross of Christ. "This man was innocent beyond doubt," he exclaims. The wording of his confession fits perfectly with Luke's portrayal of Jesus in the passion. Jesus the martyr prophet was indeed a "just" man: totally committed to God's cause; willing to face death for the sake of the gospel.

Luke also uniquely describes the impact of Jesus' death on the bystanders. The people who had walked the way of the cross with Jesus (23:27) and now witness his death return "beating their breasts"—a sign of repentance (23:48). And standing at a distance are those "who knew" Jesus (Luke's subtle way of inching the frightened and scattered disciples back into the story?) and the faithful women "who had followed him from Galilee" (23:49). The gathering of the community which would burst into life after the resurrection already begins, at the very moment of Jesus' life-giving death.

Death and Victory
(23:50-56)

The passion narrative ends on a muted note. The power of Jesus reaches beyond death as Joseph of Arimathea, whom Luke describes with his favorite terms as a "virtuous" and "righteous" man, a member of the very council who had condemned Jesus yet one who had not consented to their verdict, takes courage and comes to claim the body of Jesus for burial. In any age, claiming the body of an executed man from the authorities is a public act, exposing one's allegiances for all to see. Joseph stands clearly with the crucified Jesus.

He wraps Jesus' broken body in a linen burial cloth and places it in a rock tomb in which no one had yet been buried. Luke carefully sets the stage for the marvelous events of the resurrection. The Sabbath eve was approaching so there was no time to anoint the body. But the faithful women who had ministered to Jesus in Galilee (8:2-3) and stood by him at the moment of death (23:49) prepare spices and perfumed oil—ready to return and anoint the crucified body of Jesus as soon as the Sabbath rest was completed.

One cannot miss the touching poignancy of these details: the courageous devotion of Joseph, the faithful women who abide by the Sabbath law yet with their hearts in that tomb with the one they loved and had lost. The reader knows, however, that death will not have the last word. The "just one" would break the bonds of death and the tomb would be robbed of its treasure. The Spirit that had fallen on Jesus at the moment of his Baptism would once again pulsate within his living being as the Risen Christ would rise triumphant from death and charge his disciples to bring God's word and the witness of their lives to all nations.

THE PASSION ACCORDING TO JOHN

John's Gospel has been called the "maverick" Gospel because its portrayal of Jesus is done in a manner quite distinctive from that of Mark, Matthew and Luke. For John, Jesus is the revelation of God's love for the world, the "Word made Flesh" whose death is an act of friendship love, a sign of God's total embrace of humanity and the final triumph over evil. John's passion account is read each year as the centerpiece of the Good Friday liturgy. His portrayal of the passion, with its masterful blend of suffering and triumph, fits well into the spirit of the Paschal Triduum.

The Arrest
(18:1-11)

The opening scene of John's account sets the mood for the entire passion story. On one level, it is a tale of terror—betrayal by a friend, a violent nighttime arrest of an innocent person, the abuse of power by armed authorities. This is a chilling scene—very familiar and very contemporary for Christians in many parts of the world.

But there is another level to this scene—Jesus freely choosing to place himself before his enemies; the overwhelming authority of his sacred person hurling the powers of darkness to the ground; Jesus in command even at the moment of his arrest.

So it is with John's entire passion story: the tragedy of violent death is overwhelmed by the power of redemptive love. For John, Jesus is the Word made Flesh, sent to reveal the abiding love of God for the world. The most compelling statement of that love is, paradoxically, the death of Jesus. In giving his life "for his friends" (15:13)—the most noble of human actions—Jesus reveals God's overwhelming love for the world. From the perspective of faith, the death of Jesus is a word of life.

John's passion begins abruptly in comparison to the Synoptic gospels. There is no reference to the plot against Jesus, no anointing at Bethany and no account of the last supper, nor does Jesus pray his anguished prayer in Gethsemane before the moment of the arrest. To some degree John has taken care of these events or their equivalents earlier in his Gospel. Once Jesus has completed his long farewell discourse with the disciples (chs. 13-17), he leads them across the Kidron valley to a garden and the drama of the passion will begin (18:1).

John's account does not flinch before the terrible reality of death. It first appears in the guise of Judas, the disciple who betrays Jesus. In John's perspective, "Satan"—the very personification of evil—induces Judas to betray Jesus (13:2). Allied with Judas are Roman soldiers (only John mentions this) and guards from the priests and the Pharisees (18:3). The whole spectrum of power is arrayed against Jesus: Jew and Gentile; secular and religious.

But this phalanx of oppressive and even demonic power does not make Jesus a helpless victim. Earlier in the Gospel, the Johannine Jesus had stated his freedom in the face of death: "This is why the Father loves me, because I lay down my life in order to take it up again. No one takes it from me, but I lay it down on my own. I have power to lay it down, and power to take it up again. This command I have received from my Father" (10:17-18).

Jesus confronts the powers with his sacred name: "I AM"—the divine name which Jesus the Word reveals to the world. In the face of this, the powers of death wilt and fall to the ground—not once but twice. Jesus, not death, is in command here. He lets his disciples leave (18:8—they do not flee as in Mark and Matthew's accounts) and he restrains Peter from any violence on his behalf.

Jesus will freely and willingly "drink the cup" of the passion because in so doing he fulfills his mission of revealing God's love for the world.

In the Courtyard of the High Priest (18:12-27)

The scene now changes from the Garden across the Kidron valley to the courtyard of the high priest. In John's version of the story, Jesus is taken first to Annas, the father-in-law of the reigning high priest Caiaphas. Presumably Annas, who had been deposed by the Romans, remained a powerful figure. Jesus will be interrogated by the religious authorities in preparation for his formal trial before Pilate.

But for John the deeper motif of this scene remains one of contrasts: between Jesus and his opponents and between Jesus and Peter.

As in the arrest scene Jesus boldly confronts his opponents. In words reminiscent of chapter 8 of the Gospel, John presents Jesus as the embodiment of "truth"—the ultimate truth of God's love

for the world. Jesus has openly proclaimed this truth in his words and actions (18:20). In John's theology, truth has an inherently "public" character. Those who speak the truth or seek to discover it are not afraid to come into the light (3:19-21), but those whose lives are built on falsehood or who shy from the truth prefer to live in darkness and to operate in secret. Thus Judas and his armed band had come to arrest Jesus in the darkness (ironically, carrying lanterns and torches. . . 18:3). And so, too, the high priest fails to recognize the Truth of God that stands before him bound as a prisoner.

John also tells the story of Peter's denial. Here the contrast is between the fearless public witness that Jesus gives before his captors and the weakness of the disciple who denies his discipleship when confronted with the question of a maidservant. Peter had boldly affirmed that he would lay down his life for Jesus and insisted that he would follow Jesus wherever he would go (13:36-38). But he had underestimated the power of darkness and the cost of discipleship. In the crisis of the passion he fails.

But the Gospel does not abandon Peter. He will witness the empty tomb and ponder its meaning (20:6-9) and finally, in the exquisite story of the breakfast on the shore of the lake (ch. 21), the Risen Christ will heal Peter's broken discipleship with a threefold confession of love and entrust him with the mission of serving the community.

John also introduces a new element into this story. Peter is able to enter the courtyard because of "another disciple" known to the high priest (18:15). This is most likely the "Beloved Disciple"—that mysterious figure in John's Gospel who represents authentic discipleship. He, along with the Mother of Jesus, will be the witnesses to Jesus' death (19:26, 35-36).

John's sense of contrast and irony continues to add deep levels of meaning to the passion story: truth and falsehood, strength and weakness are revealed in the crisis moment of suffering.

Jesus before Pilate (18:28-40)

The trial of Jesus by the Roman procurator Pontius Pilate dominates the Johannine passion story. The evangelist organizes the trial into a series of vignettes, alternately staged inside the praetorium and outside in full view of the crowds. The scenes mount in intensity, beginning with Pilate's seemingly bored discussion with the religious leaders, through his increasing mystification with his prisoner, and climaxing with his attempt to free Jesus that is rejected by the crowd.

John once again injects irony into his narrative. In the first scene the religious leaders are concerned with maintaining ritual purity, but they are engaged in handing over the Son of God to the Romans. They are concerned to be ready for the feast of Passover (18:28) yet the true Passover Lamb is about to be sacrificed. Their jousting with the Roman procurator about legal rights leads ironically to Jesus being crucified—the very manner of death which the Johannine Jesus had predicted he would undergo, being "lifted up" for the life of the world (see 3:14-15; 12:32-33).

A potent symbol of the whole trial is that of kingship, a theme that emerges as Pilate begins to interrogate Jesus (18:33-38). Pilate represents political might symbolized in the emperor's crown. But Jesus' sovereignty is not "of this world," that is, it represents a very different sort of power—one that gives life. As the prologue of the Gospel had already proclaimed in poetic fashion (1:1-18) Jesus came into the world to proclaim the ultimate truth of God's love—those who hear the voice of Jesus know God's truth and live it out in their lives (8:47). The truth of God's love—and not brute, oppressive force—is the source of Jesus' power. Pilate, like the religious leaders, is incapable of recognizing this truth (18:37).

Even though he cannot understand Jesus, Pilate is convinced of his innocence and he goes outside to inform the leaders of his decision. To assuage them, he offers to release Jesus as a gesture on the occasion of the Passover (18:39). But the "Jews" demand that Barabbas be released instead. The Gospel simply notes that Barabbas was a "revolutionary" (18:40). Is John's irony at work again? Does the evangelist imply for the reader that the crowds are blind to the fact that the most profound revolution is the one inaugurated by Jesus himself?

[Note that at this point John has subtly moved from identifying Jesus' opponents as the religious leaders to calling them in generic fashion, "the Jews"—the Christian reader must be careful not to draw the conclusion that all Jews are somehow guilty for the death of Jesus. This cannot be John's point: Mary, the Beloved Disciple, and Jesus himself were Jews!]

Jesus the Crucified King (19:1-16)

The motif of Kingship intensifies in the concluding scenes. When the crowd selects Barabbas to be freed, Pilate has Jesus scourged (19:1-3). The soldiers perform a cruel coronation parody: after being beaten, Jesus is crowned with thorns, robed in purple and offered mock homage: "Hail, King of the Jews!" The mockery is punctuated with further violence as the soldiers strike him "repeatedly."

All of this prepares for the bizarre scene that follows as Pilate leads his beaten prisoner, robed in his mock royal trappings, out to the crowds. Pilate hopes this will quench their desire to have Jesus destroyed.

For Pilate and the characters in the drama, this is a complete humiliation of this royal pretender. Jesus is a buffoon, without power or following, garbed in mock symbols of royalty. But for the reader of the Gospel there is another truth. Jesus truly is "king"; he is God's royal Son. What is being mocked here is not Jesus but any crown whose power is based on violence and falsehood. Pilate presents Jesus as a pitiful "man," but the eye of faith knows that this human being is the Word made Flesh, the "Son of Man" who came down from heaven to reveal God's love for the world.

Again irony courses through John's narrative: Jesus must die, his opponents shout, "because he made himself the Son of God" (19:7). John's Gospel has proclaimed that Jesus will die precisely because he is God's Son who gives his life for the world.

Stung by the crowd's rejection of Jesus and still seeking a way to release this mysterious prisoner, Pilate again interrogates Jesus. Pilate's claim to power is brushed aside: the only power is that which God gives (19:11).

When Pilate once again pleads with the crowd on behalf of Jesus, they threaten to accuse him of disloyalty to Caesar (19:12). Once more irony drips from the words: "Everyone who makes himself a king opposes Caesar"—just so, the reader of the Gospel can say. Jesus is a king and the nature of his kingship is diametrically opposed to the abusive power that takes life from the innocent.

The scene ends with the crowds demanding Jesus be crucified. The symbolism is very strong. Pilate leads Jesus out and sits on the judgment seat. "Behold your king," he says to taunt the crowds, but they reply: "We have no king but Caesar." From the perspective of John's Gospel, Pilate is right and the Jerusalem crowds could make no more terrible choice.

The Lifting Up of the Son of Man (19:17-30)

The climax of the passion comes on Golgotha where Jesus is crucified. John's emphasis on the triumphant initiative of Jesus even in the darkest moment of the passion continues. There is no Simon of Cyrene impounded to carry the cross; the Johannine Jesus takes it up himself.

The moment of crucifixion is an enthronement: Jesus is crucified, surrounded by an improbable retinue of two others who die in the same way. Over the cross emblazoned in Hebrew,

Latin and Greek is the title: "Jesus the Nazorean, the King of the Jews." Even though the chief priests protest, Pilate is adamant—this will be the title of the Crucified Jesus.

Using the haunting symbolism of the bronze serpent from the story of Moses in Numbers 14:21 (see John 3:14), John's Gospel presented the crucifixion as a "lifting up"—that is, a triumphant exaltation as the Word made Flesh completes his mission of love and returns to the Father (13:1).

John fills this climactic scene with other potent symbols. The seamless tunic of Jesus (reminiscent of the high priest's garment? or of the unity Jesus came to create?) is not torn (19:23-24). At the brink of death, Jesus "thirsts," recalling his words to Peter in the garden: "Shall I not drink the cup that the Father gave me?" (18:11).

One other final action involves the mother of Jesus and his Beloved Disciple (19:25-27). The precise meaning of this incident is difficult to determine. Does it mean that the Beloved Disciple is now a member of Jesus' household or community ("[Son,] behold your mother")? Does the mother of Jesus symbolize Judaism and now she "gives birth" to a new community symbolized by Jesus' disciple, while at the same time, the Christian community must be respectful of its parentage in Judaism? Or does the mother of Jesus represent that great faith of Israel whose pangs of childbirth are now complete in the community of faith that begins with the death and resurrection of Jesus (see this image used in Jesus' farewell discourse, 16:21-22).

So often John's Gospel tantalizes the reader and does not dictate which range of meaning one must draw from the text.

John describes the death of Jesus in brief and bold strokes. Jesus' final words are: "It is finished" (19:30). They ring with Johannine spirit. The Greek verb used here, *teleo*, connotes "completion," "arriving at the intended goal." Jesus had set out to do the will of the Father, to love his own "until the end" (13:1, the same root word, *telos*, is used). Bowing his head in a graceful and composed manner, Jesus the Word made Flesh, hands over his life spirit to God. There is a magnificent sense of serenity and strength as the Johannine Jesus meets death. His death is no play acting (John will make that point in the spear thrust that follows), but the terror of death has been defused by love.

Testimony (19:31-42)

John's passion story concludes with two brutal acts in the ritual of crucifixion that are given new meaning by the Gospel.

The executioners come to break the legs of the crucified in order to hasten death before the Sabbath eve begins. But they do not break Jesus' legs; unwittingly they fulfill the words of Scripture in reference to the passover lamb (see, for example, Exodus 12:46). In the testimony of the Baptist earlier in the Gospel, Jesus is the "Lamb of God" who has come to take away the sins of the world (1:29, 36).

To make sure Jesus is dead, one of the soldiers drives a lance into his side.

Blood and water stream from the side of Jesus. Once again, a brutal act takes on new meaning in the eye of the Gospel. The Gospel cites Zechariah 12:10, a haunting text that speaks of the inhabitants of Jerusalem repenting and receiving God's forgiveness when they look on one "whom they have pierced." Water and blood have rich meaning in John's Gospel. In chapter 7 Jesus used the symbol of water to refer to the Spirit that would course into the world through his life-giving death (see 7:37-39). And in the bread of life discourse, Jesus had spoken of his blood that gives life to those who partake of it (6:53, 54, 55-56).

All of these signs confirm the redemptive power of Jesus' death in John's Gospel and for this reason the evangelist emphasizes the decisive testimony of the "witness" at the cross (19:35)—presumably the Beloved Disciple who was the key link between the original community of Jesus and the Johannine church.

The finale is reached as Jesus' crucified body is taken from the cross for burial. Already the effects of Jesus' mission are evident. Joseph of Arimathea, who out of fear had been a disciple only in secret, now takes courage and comes to claim the body. He is joined by Nicodemus, a Pharisee, who had first come to Jesus "at night" (3:1) and whose faith had been tentative (7:50-52). He brings an enormous amount of spices— enough for a royal burial!

Both men lay aside their fear and openly pay homage to the crucified Jesus. Those in the darkness are now coming out into the light. God's Word of love has triumphed over death.

FOR FURTHER STUDY . . .

The passion of Jesus has held the attention of the Christians throughout the ages. The Gospels themselves testify to this—each of them makes the passion the climax of their narrative and devotes an extraordinary amount of attention to this singular event. So, too, has Christian piety, art and theology throughout the centuries probed the meaning of the passion.

Contemporary scholarship is no exception. The unspeakable horror of the holocaust and the devastation of the Second World War gave new impetus to studies of the passion. Those who encouraged anti-Semitism and paved the way for genocide often appealed to Jewish responsibility for the death of Jesus as a spurious justification for their evil. Too often other Christians were mute when the gospels were used for such a demonic purpose. It was time for Christian scholars to examine their consciences and to see to what extent their portrayals of Jews at the time of Jesus and their ways of interpreting the death of Jesus had contributed to this toxic atmosphere.

In the past half century there has been a remarkable and constructive reappraisal of the Jewish roots of Christianity by Christian and Jewish scholars alike, and this has had an impact as well on the study of the gospels and the passion narrative. Extraordinary archeological discoveries have also helped us understand better the social, political and religious circumstances of Jesus' day. Jesus was thoroughly Jewish and revered his religious heritage. Not all Jews were opposed to him and there could be no collective Jewish responsibility for his death. Much of the tension between Jesus and some of the Jewish leaders in the gospels reflect not only conflicts between Jesus and his contemporaries, but later conflicts between the emerging Christian community and its Jewish counterpart at the time the gospels were being composed. These and other observations represent important gains in our understanding of history.

Modern biblical scholarship has also been attuned to the literary quality of the gospels themselves. These narratives draw on historical traditions but shape them in a manner designed to move the reader and trigger reflection. The evangelists naturally used the literary methods specific to their culture and time. The more we know about the literary structure and style of the gospels, the better we are equipped to read them with deeper understanding.

The study of the four passion accounts in this book has taken a more literary and theological approach to the gospel texts. We have probed these passion stories, not so much for what they can tell us about the precise historical circumstances of Jesus' passion, but what the meaning of the suffering and death of Jesus might be in the light of Christian faith.

The section on the history and archeology of the passion obviously moves in a more historical fashion, while the segment on devotion to the passion gives some leads on the way different periods of Christianity have reflected on the death of Jesus.

For the reader who is not a specialist yet wants to explore further some of these directions in their study of the passion, the bibliography found on page 96 might be helpful.

In Search of the Passion of Jesus

History, Archeology, and Devotion

JERUSALEM AFTER JESUS

Besides the gospel stories, do other sources shed light on the events of Jesus' Passion?

The city of Jerusalem itself, where Jesus' Passion took place, is a likely place to look. What makes our search difficult, however, is the almost complete devastation the city suffered in the Roman siege that leveled most of its walls and buildings during the Jewish revolt in 70 B.C. With brutal thoroughness the legions of the Roman general Titus destroyed the city, killing or enslaving its inhabitants. Some of the fiercest fighting took place around the traditional place of Calvary. The city was completely rebuilt by the Emperor Hadrian in the late second century.

After the Roman period, Persian, Moslem, and Crusader armies swept through the Holy Land, destroying or rebuilding on the sacred sites. For almost two thousand years, the land has suffered more than its share of wars, earthquakes and other natural disasters. The city is hardly a place one expects to find many traces of the past. Yet traces remain.

Relief on Arch of Titus in Rome: *The seven-branch lampstand and other treasures from the temple at Jerusalem are carried in triumph by Titus's legions.*

Stones from Destruction of the Temple *uncovered in the excavations of 1967.*

Palm Sunday Pilgrims *approaching Jerusalem from the Mount of Olives.*

Jerusalem Rebuilt by Hadrian

After a second Jewish revolt in 135 A.D. the Emperor Hadrian sought to obliterate all trace of the ancient city by completely rebuilding Jerusalem as a Roman city, using the plan followed by Roman builders for constructing a colony. The plan resulted in a city smaller in size than before, which can still be seen in the street-plan of present-day Jerusalem.

Renaming it "Aelia Capitolina," Hadrian repopulated his new city with foreign colonists and prohibited Jews from entering the city under pain of death. Statues of Roman gods and goddesses replaced sacred Jewish sites. Little remained, at least visibly, of Jerusalem's Jewish past except the desolate foundation of the temple.

The Jewish-Christian Community

Even so, there is some evidence that a small Jewish-Christian community continued to meet on Mount Zion in the southern outskirts of the city, though its activities were restricted. They cherished certain sites associated with the memory of Jesus: a cave at Bethlehem marking his birth, a cave near the summit of the Mount of Olives marking his last teachings to his disciples and his ascension, and the site of his death and resurrection which they placed alongside the forum in Hadrian's new city, where the Romans had raised a statue of Venus.

Their traditions, which we can categorize as pre-Constantinian (before 313 A.D.), provided the basis for later Christian identification of some key sites.

CONSTANTINE'S JERUSALEM

The face of Jerusalem dramatically changed when the Emperor Constantine began an era of toleration and favor toward the Christian church in 313 A.D. Constantine initially built three basilicas on the ancient Christian locations pointed out by tradition: Calvary, the Mount of Olives, and Bethlehem. As Christians flocked to the Holy City these locations became the principal sites of liturgical life for Jerusalem's growing Christian church, which soon influenced Christian liturgical practices and devotion throughout the world.

The Basilica of the Holy Sepulcher built by Constantine: from the 6th century mosaic map of Madaba.

From the 4th to the 7th century the Holy Land became a Christian land, a land of pilgrims, a great visual bible. Almost 500 Christian churches and shrines were built, many over places thought to commemorate incidents in the Old or New Testaments. One must recognize, however, that many sites were chosen overzealously. Scholars like St. Jerome (+ 420) who took up permanent residence near the holy places in order to study the scriptures in detail and practice the Christian life complained about the tendency of the *"monstratores,"* the guides, to multiply places and relics so that the multitude of eager pilgrims who craved to touch and see the places mentioned in the Bible could be satisfied.

In great detail, the gospel stories acquired a concrete setting. As early as 333 A.D. an anonymous pilgrim from Bordeaux in Gaul was shown on the Mount of Olives "a vineyard where there is the rock where Judas Iscariot betrayed Christ and the palmtree from which the children took branches and strewed them in Christ's path, the rock on which Christ was laid to prepare for burial."

Among the remains of Jerusalem's long history, then, are cult sites like these, still to be seen and held in veneration. They are places of prayer hallowed by a long tradition of devotion, but with only a tenuous connection to the historical site and event. For original historical value one generally looks for sites based on pre-Constantinian traditions (before 313 B.C.) rather than for traditions from the Byzantine or medieval periods.

The Church of the Holy Sepulcher: *The present church (above) stands on the site of an earlier church constructed in 335A.D. by the Emperor Constantine who, relying on ancient Christian traditions, built it over the tomb of Jesus. Pilgrimage to the site was so instantly popular that St. John Chrysostom (+ 407) remarked: "The whole world runs to see a tomb that has no body."*

Fire, earthquake, and numerous structural changes have damaged the present church which replaced the Constantinian church destroyed in 1009 A.D. Beneath its dome is the traditional location of the tomb of Christ. Underneath the church's smaller dome is the traditional site of Calvary.

THE JERUSALEM TEMPLE

The temple in Jerusalem, brilliantly restored and expanded by Herod the Great (+ 4 B.C.) played a key role in Jewish religious, political and economic life at the time of Jesus. Its massive walls and buildings dominated the city itself; during the great Jewish feasts it was a magnet drawing Jews from beyond the city and from all over the world, who tripled Jerusalem's existing population. Ever sensitive to possible danger from a volatile mix of religious fervor and revolutionary politics at such times, Pontius Pilate, the Roman procurator, left his administrative center at Caesarea Maritima and came to Jerusalem with extra troops to maintain order and act quickly in case of trouble. Some of those troops were stationed at the Fortress Antonia adjacent to the temple.

The gospels report that Jesus came to Jerusalem to celebrate the feast of the Passover. He taught regularly in the temple area, and his teaching gravely concerned the rulers of the city. On one occasion, he upset the tables of the temple vendors which further provoked the city's religious leaders. Those actions

Temple Column: *Once part of Herod's great building.*

were a major factor leading to his condemnation and death.

Today nothing remains of the temple and its surrounding buildings which were destroyed by the Roman legions of Titus in 70 A.D. except some broken pieces and the great platform created as the site for the temple by Herod the Great. Now that site is dominated by the impressive Moslem shrine, the Dome of the Rock, built after the Moslem conquest of Palestine in the 7th century, which presides over Jerusalem's skyline today.

The Temple as Reconstructed: *Its innermost room was the Holy of Holies. In the surrounding porticoes, people congregated and listened to teachers and rabbis. Jesus and the apostles taught there. On the left, the Royal portico where the moneychangers' tables stood and animals and birds were sold for sacrifice. On the right, the towers of the Antonia fortress, rebuilt by Herod the Great and used by the Romans to control Jerusalem, especially the temple area. (Model of Jerusalem: Holy Land Hotel.)*

Southern Side of the Temple: *from the Holy Land Hotel model.*

The Temple Steps: The Southern side of the Temple

Excavations begun on the southern side of the temple platform in 1967 revealed parts of the original great stairway of thirteen steps leading to the southern entrances of the temple as well as ritual baths for purification that visitors used before they went to worship. Since this entrance was the main entrance for pilgrims, it is likely Jesus and his disciples walked these steps.

Temple Steps: *Visitors walking the ancient steps.*

Approach to Gethsemane

On a path such as this, Jesus and his disciples, according to the gospels, descended from the city after the meal into the Kidron Valley and walked to the garden called Gethsemane to the north-east.

The Kidron Valley, filled with tombs today as in the time of Jesus, offered a stark reminder of death. It was a favorite burial place for pious Jews, not only because of its proximity to the temple area (left in picture) but also because of the belief that the Valley of Jehoshaphat, the place where the Lord will judge the nations according to the Prophet Joel (3:2) was identical with the Kidron ravine.

Sites of the Passion of Jesus: *Southern approach to the Mount of Olives.*

THE MOUNT OF OLIVES

Arrest of Jesus: *Detail from the Church at Gethsemane.*

Part of the two and a half mile long mountain ridge that faces Jerusalem and the Kidron Valley from the east, the Mount of Olives attracted Christians both in pre-Constantinian times and later because of its many associations with Jesus. Approaching from Jericho in the east, Jesus must have had his first view of the city of Jerusalem from here. He stayed with friends at nearby Bethany on a southeastern portion of this mountain range (Jn 12:1; Mt 21:17-18; Mk 11:11-12), and there he raised Lazarus from the dead (Jn 11). He taught his disciples on the Mount of Olives (Mt 24:1—26:2) and riding on a colt he entered Jerusalem from here (Mt 21:1-9). According to the Acts of the Apostles (1:6-12), Jesus ascended into heaven from here.

On the western slope of the Mount of Olives, Jesus fell into an agony, prayed, and was arrested by the authorities.

Eusebius, the bishop of Caesarea, writing about 300 A.D., confirms the importance of the Mount of Olives to Christian pilgrims from earliest times:

"All who believe in Christ come here to Jerusalem from every part of the world, not as in the past to admire the splendor of the city or to pray at the temple, but to wonder at the effects of the conquest and destruction of Jerusalem and to pray on the Mount of Olives opposite the city . . . where the Savior's feet rested " (*Dem.* VI, 18, 23).

By the end of the 6th century over twenty-four Christian churches were built on this mountain, which had become the home of thousands of monks and nuns.

The Mount of Olives: *The triple-arched Church of All Nations, the third church in a series built on the spot tradition holds to be the place where Jesus' agony, prayer and arrest took place, is midpoint in the picture.*

The Garden of Gethsemane: *an ancient olive tree. The trees, though very old, are later than those of Jesus' time.*

The Church at Gethsemane

The Church at Gethsemane, called "The Church of all Nations," was built in 1924 on the site where from the 4th century three previous churches marked the place where Jesus prayed. An area of open bare rock within the church honors the place of Jesus's prayer.

Because it is located along the natural route from Jerusalem to Bethany, the present site, recognized by Christians from pre-Constantinian times, is a likely place for the events the gospels describe.

The Kidron Valley: *with its expanse of tombs, seen from Gethsemane. A natural passage for Jesus on the way to the garden.*

THE UPPER CITY

After Jesus' arrest in the Garden of Gethsemane, where was he taken? The gospels say it was "to Annas, the father-in-law of Caiaphas" (Jn 18:12-13) "to Caiaphas" (Mt 26:57) or "to the high priest" (Mk 14:53) or "to the high priest's house" (Lk 22:54). Most likely the place was somewhere in Jerusalem's Upper City, where influential Jews of Jesus' day lived in large splendid houses, many built during Herod the Great's massive reconstruction of the city.

Connected directly to the temple by a viaduct over the Tyropoean Valley, the Upper City was a convenient home for families and officials with temple duties. Recently archeologists have excavated some of these homes, constructed in the style of 1st century Roman villas, with courtyards and elegant furnishings. Like the rest of Jerusalem, the Upper City was destroyed by fire in the Roman siege of 70 A.D.

After the city was rebuilt on a smaller scale by Hadrian in the 2nd century, there is evidence of a small Jewish-Christian church located in the southerly outskirts of Aelia Capitolina, called by Christians, "Mount Zion." Early Christian traditions mark this as the place of

Ancient stairway: *to the Upper City.*

Pentecost, the upper room, where the Holy Spirit descended on the apostles after Jesus' resurrection. Somewhat later it was honored as the Cenacle where Jesus ate the Last Supper. By the 4th century the house of Caiaphas was also located in this vicinity. Today the modern church of the Dormition is the most prominent Christian shrine marking the ancient Christian "Mount Zion."

The Northwest Section of Ancient Jerusalem Today: *Remains of Herod's palace in Jerusalem's Upper City can be seen in the lower right hand corner of the picture. The church of the Holy Sepulcher, identified by its large and small dome, is seen at the bottom left of the picture. In the distance (upper part of the photograph), the temple mount and the Mount of Olives beyond.*

Upper City: *from Herod's palace eastward to the temple and the Fortress Antonia. (From the model: Holy Land Hotel.)*

Where was Jesus judged by Pilate?

Jesus "was crucified under Pontius Pilate," the Roman Procurator. The credal statement summarizes the gospel report: Jesus, while in Jerusalem to celebrate the Passover, was condemned to death by Pontius Pilate, who represented Roman authority in Judea.

Traditions point out three sites where this judgment may have taken place. All three were major administrative and military locations built or renovated by Herod the Great (+ 4 A.D.) in his massive reconstruction of the city. During the time of Jesus they were used by the Roman authorities.

Herod's Upper Palace *(Picture: fore-ground)*, the most magnificent of the three, and perhaps the most likely place for Pilate to reside in Jerusalem, was built around 24 B.C. on the strategic southwestern hill of the city protected by the city wall to the west and three large towers on its northern flank. A large wall separated the opulent palace from a city forum to the east. Entering the forum, Pilate set up his judgment seat and sentenced Jesus to death before the crowd, which would not enter the palace precincts for fear of incurring ritual impurity. Afterwards, he gave Jesus to the soldiers, whose barracks probably adjoined the palace to the north. They scourged him and then led him through the nearby gate to Calvary.

Herod's Lower Palace *(Picture: twin towers, upper right)*, formerly the Hasmonean Palace, was located near the bridge connecting the Upper City with the temple enclosure. Many early Christian traditions point it out as the place where Jesus was judged.

The Fortress Antonia *(Picture: upper center)*, was built by Herod in the northwestern corner of the temple area to provide security in that important place. From the time of the Crusaders (12th century) this site was usually considered the place of judgment, but today a better understanding of the topography and times of first-century Jerusalem has led experts to favor Herod's Upper Palace as the place where Pilate sentenced Jesus.

Pilate's Inscription; *Caesarea Maritima.*

Pontius Pilate

In 1961 Italian archeologists discovered, in Caesarea Maritima, a fragmentary inscription carrying the name of Pontius Pilate. Caesarea Maritima was the usual residence of the Roman authorities in Judea. They would come to Jerusalem only on occasions, such as a religious feast.

In full, the inscription states that Pilate, the Procurator of Judea from 26 to 36 A.D., dedicated a temple in honor of Tiberius.

CALVARY

Crucifixion, called by ancient writers the harshest of deaths, was commonly employed by the Romans at the time of Jesus to punish and execute slaves and rebels.

After being sentenced, the victim usually was made to carry to the place of execution either the crossbeam or the cross itself. Flogging and other forms of torture added by the executioners were part of the cruel process. The unusually swift death of Jesus, which the gospels report, may have been caused by the severity of these preliminary punishments.

The Romans used various methods of crucifixion. Following a common

method, which Jesus probably experienced, the victim was first stripped of his clothes and then fixed to the crossbeam with nails that passed through

Sketch of crucifixion as practiced by Romans.

the bones of his arm below the wrist. Then his body was seated to a small wooden peg jutting from the upright beam to which his heels were nailed (below left). As his body weight closed his breathing passages, the victim died of suffocation, sometimes after days of bitter pain. Hanging close to the ground the victim sometimes was the prey of dogs and birds.

In June, 1968, the bones of a young man (above) who appears to have been crucified about the time of Jesus were discovered at Giv'at ha-Mivtar near Jerusalem. His heels seem to have been nailed to a cross, with the iron nail still piercing his heelbone.

Calvary (Hypothetically Reconstructed), *the skull-shaped mound, seen left foreground in the sketch, was located in the northwest section of the city near the gate, adjacent to a limestone quarry where Jesus was buried in a tomb after his crucifixion. Some years later an extension of the city walls brought the site within the city itself and burials ceased.*

Herod's Palace and the Towers *dominating the city from high position are seen right foreground. There Jesus was judged by Pilate, who made his residence at the palace during important Jewish feasts. From there he was led to Calvary, a short distance away.*

Sketch of a Jewish tomb from the time of Jesus.

THE TOMB OF JESUS

Burial. A good number of tombs from the time of Jesus have been discovered around Jerusalem, and so burial practices of the day can be described with some accuracy. It was customary then to place the body, washed, anointed with oils and spices and wrapped in a shroud, in the family tomb where it was placed either in a shaft cut into the rock, or on a shelf cut laterally into the rock under a vaulted arch (see illustration above). Then, after the flesh had decayed, the bones were gathered and placed in a stone box called an ossuary.

The entrance to the tomb was often sealed with a heavy rolling stone to prevent animals from invading the tomb.

According to the gospels, Jesus' body was buried hurriedly before the Sabbath by Joseph of Arimathea in a tomb close by the place of crucifixion. Some women followers of Jesus, knowing where he was buried, were intent on returning after the Sabbath to complete the burial process. When they did, they found the tomb empty.

Tombs from 1st Century: *Excavations begun in the 1960's beneath the church of the Holy Sepulcher, close by the place where the tomb of Christ is revered, uncovered tombs dating from the 1st century (above) and evidence that the area had once been a limestone quarry.*

The Tomb of Christ, in the Church of the Holy Sepulcher:
Covered with a marble top the limestone shelf that tradition points out as the resting place of the body of Jesus has been a sacred place of Christian pilgrimage for over sixteen hundred years.

The Sea of Galilee: *After rising from the dead, Jesus appeared to his disciples on the shores of the Sea of Galilee (Jn 21).*

THE STATIONS OF THE CROSS

Jerusalem pilgrims beginning the Stations of the Cross.

One Christian tradition, well known to generations of Jerusalem pilgrims, is the devotion of the Stations of the Cross. The devotion likely began, according to some historians, with the practice of early Byzantine pilgrims who on Holy Thursday went in procession from Gethsemane on the eastern side of Jerusalem westward to the church of the Holy Sepulcher. By the 18th century the route became known as the Via Dolorosa.

From the 14th century, pilgrims under the guidance of the Franciscans commemorated the journey of Jesus to Calvary along this route, with specific locations gradually marked for incidents of the journey. From Jerusalem the devotion of the Stations of the Cross spread to churches and shrines in western Christianity where it influenced popular Christian reflection on the Passion of Jesus.

The Via Dolorosa in Jerusalem today begins at the remains of the fortress Antonia and proceeds westward through the streets of Jerusalem to the church of the Holy Sepulcher. Archeologists, however, generally place Jesus' judgment by Pilate at Herod's palace on the other side of the city rather than at the Antonia. From Herod's palace Jesus was led to Calvary nearby.

Whatever archeological judgments may be, the devotion of the Stations of the Cross remains a powerful form for meditating on the mystery of the passion of Jesus Christ. Based substantially on St. Luke's account of Jesus' final journey (cf. pp. 26-28) it provides a simple symbolic framework for following in the steps of Jesus.

The Via Dolorosa *in Jerusalem.*

DEVOTIONAL WRITINGS

St. Bridget of Sweden (1303-1373), one of the most influential devotional writers on the Passion of Jesus in the western church, is pictured in this 15th century woodcut writing her *Revelations,* accounts of her visions of the life, death and resurrection of Jesus. Symbols of pilgrimages she made to Rome and the Holy Land surround her.

Along with other devotional writings such as the 13th century *Meditations on the Life of Christ,* Bridget's writings had enormous influence on the Passion story in medieval art, devotion and popular religion and even today affect the way western Christians imagine the Passion of Jesus. Her writings, often adding details and visual dimensions of the Passion story not found in the gospels, invited Christians to be eyewitnesses of gospel events like the Passion of Jesus. She writes about the sacred events "as they occurred or as they might have occurred according to the devout belief of the imagination and the varying interpretation of the mind" *(Meditations).* Her purpose was not primarily to give an accurate historical account but rather to engage her readers spiritually in the mystery of their Lord. Like her, other spiritual and devotional writers have written with warmth, imagination and insight about this mystery.

Jesus scourged: *A popular medieval scene influenced by St. Bridget's* Revelations. *Mary, the mother of Jesus, watches her Son tormented.*

The church views Bridget's writings and the writings of other devotional writers with a cautious respect, neither accepting them as a totally true in every detail, nor denying their power to move hearts and minds. The words of Pope Benedict XIV probably best sum up the Church's position on writings like Bridget's: "Even though many of these revelations have been approved, we cannot and ought not give them the assent of Catholic faith, but only that of human faith, when the rules of prudence present them as probable and worthy of pious credence."

St. Bridget of Sweden writing her visions and revelations.

BIBLIOGRAPHY

1. The Historical Setting of the Passion:

Martin Hengel, *Crucifixion* (Philadelphia: Fortress, 1977). Studies the function and meaning of this form of capital punishment in Roman law.

Frederick J. Murphy, *The Religious World of Jesus* (Nashville: Abingdon, 1991). A fine introduction to the Judaism of Jesus' day.

Donald Senior, *Jesus: A Gospel Portrait* (New York: Paulist, rev. ed., 1992). A study of the historical Jesus, including the circumstances of his death.

2. Archeological Studies:

Dan Bahat, "Does the Holy Sepulcher Church Mark the Burial of Jesus?" *Biblical Archaeology Review* 12 (1986) 26-45. A good survey of this much debated question.

Gabriel Barkaky, "The Garden Tomb—Was Jesus Buried Here?" *Biblical Archaeology Review* 12 (1986) 40-57.

Jack Finegan, *The Archaeology of the New Testament* (Princeton University Press: Princeton, 1992). A fine presentation with copious illustrations.

Joseph Fitzmyer, "Crucifixion in Palestine, Qumran, and the New Testament," *The Catholic Biblical Quarterly* 40 (1978) 493-513.

Jerome Murphy-O'Connor, O.P. *The Holy Land: An Archaeological Guide from Earliest Times to 1700* (New York: Oxford University Press, 3rd ed., 1992). A guidebook and a good succinct summary of the archeological facts about different sites.

Hershal Shanks, *Jerusalem: An Archaeological Biography* (New York: Random House, 1995). A beautifully illustrated summary of the archeological evidence for each period of Jerusalem's history, including a chapter on Jerusalem at the time of Jesus.

Robert L. Wilkin, *The Land Called Holy: Palestine in Christian History and Thought* (New Haven: Yale University Press, 1992). A historical and theological reflection on the phenomenon of Christian pilgrimage, particularly to the site of Jesus' death and burial.

John Wilkinson, *Jerusalem as Jesus Knew It: Archaeology as Evidence* (London: Thames and Hudson, 1978). Especially good on the question of whether the Holy Sepulcher was the actual site of Jesus' death and burial.

3. On the Passion in the New Testament:

Raymond E. Brown, S.S., *The Death of the Messiah* (2 volumes; New York: Doubleday, 1994). A massive resource that studies the passion accounts from the Gethsemane scene to the burial. Although it is not intended as a major focus, the author also takes up many historical issues.

John T. Carroll and Joel B. Green, *The Death of Jesus in Early Christianity* (Peabody, MA: Hendrickson, 1995). Views the passion as reflected in all of the New Testament writings from both history and theology.

Frank J. Matera, *Passion Narratives and Gospel Theologies* (New York: Paulist, 1986). A study of the passion narratives in the Synoptic Gospels.

Donald Senior, C.P., *The Passion of Jesus in the Gospel of Mark* (Collegeville: Liturgical Press, 1984); *The Passion of Jesus in the Gospel of Matthew* (Collegeville: Liturgical Press, 1985); *The Passion of Jesus in the Gospel of Luke* (Collegeville: Liturgical Press, 1989); *The Passion of Jesus in the Gospel of John* (Collegeville: Liturgical Press, 1991). Each of these four volumes study the passion narratives in the context of each gospel, concentrating on the meaning of the passion.

Gerard S. Sloyan, *The Crucifixion of Jesus: History, Myth, Faith* (Minneapolis: Fortress, 1995). Studies the passion in the context of the Scriptures and as it has been interpreted in subsequent Christian history.